plurall
Parabéns!
Agora você faz parte do **Plurall**, a plataforma digital do seu livro didático!
Acesse e conheça todos os recursos e funcionalidades disponíveis para as suas aulas digitais.
Baixe o aplicativo do **Plurall** para Android e IOS ou acesse **www.plurall.net** e cadastre-se utilizando o seu código de acesso exclusivo:
CB027774
AAAEKZUXR
Este é o seu código de acesso Plurall. Cadastre-se e ative-o para ter acesso aos conteúdos relacionados a esta obra.
@plurallnet
@plurallnetoficial
SOMOS
EDUCAÇÃO

COLE OS ADESIVOS NA CAPA DO LIVRO.

ENSINO FUNDAMENTAL • ANOS INICIAIS

Eliete Canesi Morino

Graduada em Língua e Literatura Inglesa e Tradução e Interpretação pela Pontifícia Universidade Católica de São Paulo (PUC-SP).

Especialização em Língua Inglesa pela International Bell School of London.

Pós-graduada em Metodologia da Língua Inglesa pela Faculdade de Tecnologia e Ciência (FTC-SP).

Atuou como professora da rede particular de ensino e em projetos comunitários.

Rita Brugin de Faria

Graduada pela Faculdade de Arte Santa Marcelina e pela Faculdade Paulista de Arte, ambas em São Paulo (SP).

Especialização em Língua Inglesa pela International Bell School of London.

Pós-graduada em Metodologia da Língua Inglesa pela Faculdade de Tecnologia e Ciência (FTC-SP).

Especialista em alfabetização, atuou como professora e coordenadora pedagógica das redes pública e particular de ensino.

Áudios

Escaneie o *QR Code* para ter acesso aos áudios deste volume e do *reader* que o acompanha.

editora ática

Presidência: Mario Ghio Júnior

Vice-presidência de educação digital: Camila Montero Vaz Cardoso

Direção editorial: Lidiane Vivaldini Olo

Gerência editorial: Julio Cesar Augustus de Paula Santos

Coordenação editorial: Luciana Nicoleti

Edição: Ana Lucia Militello

Aprendizagem digital: Renata Galdino (ger.), Beatriz de Almeida Pinto Rodrigues da Costa (coord. de Experiência de aprendizagem), Carla Isabel Ferreira Reis (coord. de Produção multimídia), Daniela dos Santos Di Nubila (coord. de Produção digital), Rogerio Fabio Alves (coord. de Publicação) e Vanessa Tavares Menezes de Souza (coord. de Design digital)

Planejamento, controle de produção e indicadores: Flávio Matuguma (ger.), Juliana Batista (coord.) e Jayne Ruas (analista)

Revisão: Letícia Pieroni (coord.), Aline Cristina Vieira, Anna Clara Razvickas, Carla Bertinato, Daniela Lima, Danielle Modesto, Diego Carbone, Elane Vicente, Kátia S. Lopes Godoi, Lilian M. Kumai, Malvina Tomáz, Marília H. Lima, Patricia Rocco S. Renda, Paula Freire, Paula Rubia Baltazar, Paula Teixeira, Raquel A. Taveira, Ricardo Miyake, Shirley Figueiredo Ayres, Tayra Alfonso e Thaise Rodrigues

Arte: Fernanda Costa e Silva (ger.), Catherine Saori Ishihara (coord.) e Karina Vizeu Winkaler (edição de arte)

Diagramação: Ilê Comunicação Eireli

Iconografia e tratamento de imagem: Roberta Bento (ger.), Claudia Bertolazzi (coord.), Roberta Freire Lacerda dos Santos (pesquisa iconográfica), Iron Mantovanello Oliveira e Fernanda Crevin (tratamento de imagens)

Licenciamento de conteúdo de terceiros: Roberta Bento (ger.), Jenis Oh (coord.) e Liliane Rodrigues (analista de licenciamento)

Ilustrações: Clau Souza, Estudio Ornitorrinco, Ilustra Cartoon, Marcos Mello, Sirayama e Superludico

Cartografia: Eric Fuzii (coord.) e Robson da Rocha (edição de arte)

Design: Erik Taketa (coord.) e Talita Guedes da Silva (capa e proj. gráfico)

Ilustração da capa e logotipo: Superludico

Dados Internacionais de Catalogação na Publicação (CIP)

Faria, Rita Brugin de
Hello! Kids 5º ano / Rita Brugin de Faria, Eliete Canesi Morino. -- 6. ed. -- São Paulo : Ática, 2023.

Suplementado pelo manual do professor.
Bibliografia
ISBN 978-85-0819-855-9 (aluno)
ISBN 978-85-0819-848-1 (professor)

1. Lingua inglesa (Ensino fundamental) I. Morino, Eliete Canesi II. Titulo

22-0177 CDD 372.652

Angélica Ilacqua – Bibliotecária – CRB-8/7057

Dados Internacionais de Catalogação na Publicação (CIP)

Faria, Rita Brugin de
Hello! Kids 5º ano [livro eletrônico] / Rita Brugin de Faria, Eliete Canesi Morino. -- 1. ed. -- São Paulo : Ática, 2023.
PDF

Suplementado pelo manual do professor.
Bibliografia
ISBN 978-85-0819-843-6 (e-book) (aluno)
ISBN 978-85-0819-840-5 (e-book) (professor)

1. Lingua inglesa (Ensino fundamental) I. Morino, Eliete Canesi II. Titulo

22-0182 CDD 372.652

Angélica Ilacqua – Bibliotecária – CRB-8/7057

2022
6ª edição
1ª impressão
De acordo com a BNCC.

2022

Impressão e acabamento

Oceano Indústria Gráfica e Editora Ltda
CNPJ: 67.795.906/0001-10
Rua Osasco, 644 - Rod. Anhanguera, Km 33
CEP 07753-040 - Cajamar - SP

Uma publicação 

WELCOME, STUDENTS!

LET'S LEARN ENGLISH WITH HELLO! KIDS 5

Ilustrações: Clau Souza/Arquivo da editora

Marcos Mello/Arquivo da editora

CONTENTS

UNIT	CONTEMPORARY THEMES (CT) AND ENGLISH LANGUAGE COMPETENCES (ELC)	CONTENTS	VALUES	TIME TO LEARN ABOUT (CLIL)
UNIT 6 A birthday party (Birthday parties, party supplies, food and drinks, friendship) p. 82	Educação ambiental, Educação alimentar e nutricional e Vida familiar e social	• Balloons, birthday hat, blow out candles, cake, sandwiches, sweets. • Dance, greet guests, open gifts, play games, sing Happy Birthday, talk to friends. • January, February, March, April, May, June, July, August, September, October, November, December. • Ordinal numbers: 1-31. • The first day of January /January 1st (January the first). • What is your address? / When is your birthday? / Where is the party?	Friendship	——
	Review from Units 5 and 6 p. 96			
UNIT 7 A cultural fair (Countries, nationalities and languages) p. 98	Vida familiar e social, Diversidade cultural, Direitos das crianças e dos adolescentes ELC: General: 5 / English Language: 6	• Australia, Brazil, Canada, China, England, India, Japan, New Zealand, Portugal, Russia, South Africa, The United States of America. • American, Australian, Brazilian, Canadian, Chinese, English, Indian, Japanese, New Zealander, Portuguese, Russian, South African. • In, on, next to, under, behind, between. • Where are you from? / Where is Brazil? • What's your nationality? / I'm Brazilian.	Yes to cultural diversity!	Festivals of the world (Social Studies)
UNIT 8 You can help the planet (Daily sustainable actions to help the planet and the environment) p. 112	Vida familiar e social e Educação ambiental	• Cleaning, drawing, drinking, eating, playing video game, reading, resting, running, sleeping, switching on/off, talking, turning on/off, waking up, walking, washing the hands, watching TV, working, writing. • What are you doing? / I am eating a sandwich and drinking orange juice.	Protect the environment!	——
	Review from Units 7 and 8 p. 126			

Extra practice p. 128
Projects p. 144
Glossary p.152
Structures p. 159
Workbook p. 161
Celebration crafts p. 177
• Happy Easter! p. 177
• Happy Friendship Day! p. 179
• Happy Mother's Day! p. 179
• Happy Father's Day! p. 181
• Happy Thanksgiving Day! p. 181
• Merry Christmas and Happy New Year! p. 183
Mini cards p. 185
Stickers p. 193

Icons

Act Out

Check

Circle

Color
Count

Cut
Draw

Glue

Let's Talk

Listen

Make an X

Match
Number

Point

Read

Say

Sing
Stick

Workbook

Write

WELCOME!

1. Read and check the correct answers.

Question 1

START

1 How are you today?

a) Thank you.
b) I'm fine, thanks!
c) I'm late.

2 Where are your grandmother and grandfather?

a) They are in the kitchen.
b) I'm in my bedroom.
c) They are my family.

3 Where is the refrigerator?

a) It's in the bedroom.
b) It's in the living room.
c) It's in the kitchen.

4 What is your favorite food?

a) I like soda, please.
b) I'm hungry. What's for breakfast?
c) Healthy food is my favorite! I love salad and fish!

5 How can we go to school?

a) It's six blocks from here.
b) Good idea! Let's go to the new fast-food place.
c) By car or by bus.

6 Where is the subway station?

a) It's in the pet shop.
b) Three blocks from the bus stop.
c) How about going to the new shopping mall?

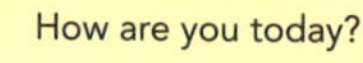

Marcos Mello/Arquivo da editora

7
What do you usually do in the morning?
a I brush my teeth, have a shower and go to school.
b I have dinner and go to sleep.
c I watch TV at 9 p.m.
8
What time is it?
a I usually do my homework at 3:00 p.m.
b It's Monday!
c It's 8:30 a.m. I'm late for school!
9
What is his job?
a He is a musician.
b I am a mechanic and she is a pilot.
c They are lawyers.
10
Is Miss Polly Jones a teacher?
a Yes, I am a teacher.
b Yes, she is a teacher.
c Yes, they are teachers.
11
What are the kids wearing?
a It's summer.
b OK! Let's pack the bags.
c Jeans, T-shirt and sneakers.
12
Why are you wearing a coat?
a Because I'm happy.
b Because it's cold. It's winter.
c Because it's summer.
FINISH
Game Quiz!
12: Awesome!
10–11: Good job!
8–9: Focus on the questions.
6-7: You can do better.
0–5: Try to solve your doubts.

UNIT 1

WHAT'S YOUR FAVORITE SUBJECT?

1. Listen and act out.  

	MONDAY
First class	Math
Second class	Robotics
Third class	Science
Fourth class	Social Studies
Fifth class	Geography
	Lunch
Sixth class	Art
Seventh class	Reading
Eighth class	Writing

FINDING OUT

2. Listen and read Jason's school schedule.  

Talking about Summers-Bell School

This is the daily schedule of the 5th and 6th graders of Jason's class.

At Summers-Bell School the school year starts in September and ends in the last week of May.

Summers-Bell School is in New York, U.S.A.

Weekly schedule for this school year:

	MONDAY	TUESDAY	WEDNESDAY	THURSDAY	FRIDAY
8:30 a.m.	Math	Math	Art	Math	Robotics
9:30 a.m.	Math	Math	Art	Math	Robotics
10:30 a.m.	Science	Language Arts	Math	Language Arts	Language Arts
11:30 a.m.	Science	Language Arts	Math	Language Arts	Language Arts
12:30 p.m.	Lunch/Recess	Lunch/Recess	Lunch/Recess	Lunch/Recess	Lunch/Recess
1:30 p.m.	Social Studies	P. E.	Language Arts	Music	Science
2:30-3:30 p.m.	Social Studies	P. E.	Language Arts	Music	Science

3. Write **True** or **False**.

a) P. E. is only on Thursdays and Wednesdays. ____________

b) Lunch is not at eleven a.m. ____________

c) Classes start at 8:00 a.m. ____________

d) Science is on Mondays, Wednesdays, Thursdays and Fridays. ____________

e) The end of the school day is at 3:30 p.m. ____________

4. Write your school schedule for this year. 

5. Listen, stick and say.

My favorite place at school is the...

6. Break the code. Guess Leo's favorite school subjects.

✠	★	✌	☞	✆	✏	✿	✂	☛	➳	✢	✦	♥
A	B	C	D	E	F	G	H	I	J	K	L	M

✈	✘	▲	❄	✸	☎	✳	✾	➵	♣	◗	✪	✉
N	O	P	Q	R	S	T	U	V	W	X	Y	Z

✿	✆	✘	✿	✸	✠	▲	✂	✪

☎	✌	☛	✆	✈	✌	✆

▲	✂	✪	☎	☛	✌	✠	✦		✆	☞	✾	✌	✠	✳	☛	✘	✈

What are Leo's favorite school subjects?

They are ____.

7. Write your favorite school subjects.

Monday	Tuesday	Wednesday
____________	____________	____________
____________	____________	____________
Thursday	**Friday**	**Saturday**
____________	____________	____________
____________	____________	____________

8. Listen and complete the numbers.  

0	zero	13	thirteen	26	twenty-six
1	one	14	________	27	twenty-seven
2	two	15	fifteen	28	twenty-________
3	three	16	sixteen	29	twenty-nine
4	four	17	________ teen	30	thirty
5	five	18	eighteen	40	forty
6	six	19	________	50	fifty
7	seven	20	twenty	60	sixty
8	eight	21	twenty-one	70	seventy
9	nine	22	twenty-________	80	eighty
10	ten	23	twenty-three	90	ninety
11	eleven	24	twenty-four	100	one hundred
12	twelve	25	________	1,000	one thousand

9. Write the numbers. 

+ plus • − minus • × times • : divided by • = equal

a) 9 × 10 = ________________

b) 36 : ________________ = 12

c) 25 + 43 = ________________

d) 6 × 9 = ________________

e) 100 − ________________ = 75

f) 22 × 4 = ________________

g) 88 : 4 = ________________

h) 4 + 3 + 6 = ________________

LISTENING AND ORAL PRACTICE

10. Listen and number.  

Ilustra Cartoon/Arquivo da editora

11. Act out and play.  

Teacher: Good morning, class!
Students: Good morning, teacher!
Teacher: I'm Mark Ford. I'm your English teacher.
Students: Nice to meet you, Mr. Ford.
Teacher: Nice to meet you, too.
Students: Welcome, Mr. Ford!
Teacher: Thanks, students!

Monkey Business Images/Shutterstock

LANGUAGE ACTIVITIES

There to be

Affirmative form	Negative Form	Interrogative Form
There is a pen on the desk.	There isn't (is not) a pen on the desk.	Is there a pen on the desk?
There are pens on the desk.	There aren't (are not) pens on the desk.	Are there pens on the desk?

12. Complete.

Ilustra Cartoon/Arquivo da editora

English | Portuguese | Math | History

How many books are there in the bookcase?

a) There ___is one___ Portuguese book in the bookcase.

b) There ______________ Math books in the bookcase.

c) There ______________ English books in the bookcase.

d) There ________ only ________ History book in the bookcase.

e) ________ there Geography books in the bookcase?

No, there ______________.

f) There _______ an Art book in the bookcase.

To Be (Affirmative Form)	
I **am**	He, She, It **is**
You **are**	We, You, They **are**

13. Read and complete with **am, is, are.**  

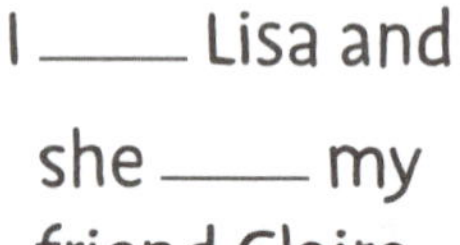

I ____ Lisa and she ____ my friend Claire.

We ____ at school.

It ____ recess time!

We have apples. They ____ delicious!
CAFETERIA

Estúdio Ornitorrinco/Arquivo de editora

14. In pairs, choose the correct answer.  

It's Geography. • It's on Friday. • There are forty.

a) How many students are there in your classroom?

____

b) When is the English class?

____

c) What is your favorite subject?

____

Pressmaster/Shutterstock

Now, ask a classmate.

Name:	Favorite school subject:
______________________	______________________

Text

Marymont School Students' Favorite Subjects

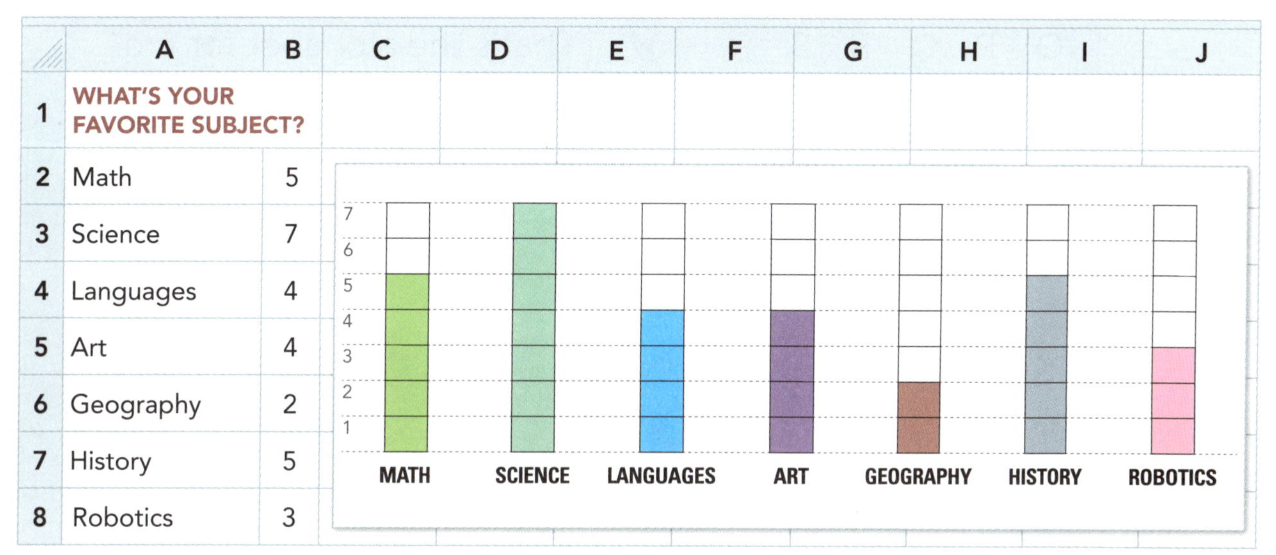

	A	B	C	D	E	F	G	H	I	J
1	WHAT'S YOUR FAVORITE SUBJECT?									
2	Math	5								
3	Science	7								
4	Languages	4								
5	Art	4								
6	Geography	2								
7	History	5								
8	Robotics	3								

15. Look at the chart and check. 

a) ◯ There are eleven students in this class.

b) ◯ Science is the favorite subject.

c) ◯ Five students like Art.

d) ◯ Three students prefer Robotics.

16. Now, you. 

	A	B	C	D	E	F	G	H	I	J
1	WHAT'S YOUR FAVORITE SUBJECT?									
2	Math									
3	Science									
4	Languages									
5	Art									
6	Geography									
7	History									
8	Robotics									

7
6
5
4
3
2
1
MATH SCIENCE LANGUAGES ART GEOGRAPHY HISTORY ROBOTICS

LET'S SING!

The Alphabet Rap

A B C D E F G
H I J K L M N
O P Q R S
T U V W
X Y Z

Start with A and end with Z.
That's the alphabet for me.

17. Make 2 new stanzas for this song.

A is for apple, B is for ball,
C is for ____________, D is for ____________,
E is for ____________, F is for ____________,
G is for ____________, H is for ____________,
I is for ____________, J is for ____________,
K is for ____________, L is for ____________,
M is for ____________, N is for ____________,
O is for ____________, P is for ____________,
Q is for ____________, R is for ____________,
S is for ____________, T is for ____________,
U is for ____________, V is for ____________,
W is for ____________, X is for ____________,
Y is for ____________, Z is for ____________.

Say with Me!

Let's spell my name: K-I-D-D-I-E F-I-V-E
Kiddie5! Kiddie5! Hurray!!!

18. Read the sentences and talk to your classmates. 

1. Come to school every day.
2. Pay attention to classes.
3. Participate in all activities.
4. Follow all school rules.
5. Always try to do your best.

19. Read and check your points.  

	Always	Sometimes	Never
1. Come to school every day.			
2. Pay attention to classes.			
3. Participate in all activities.			
4. Follow all school rules.			
5. Always try to do my best.			
Total points			

1 = very bad 2 = bad 3 = not so good 4 = good 5 = excellent

CHECK YOUR PROGRESS

AWESOME!

GOOD JOB!

I CAN DO BETTER.

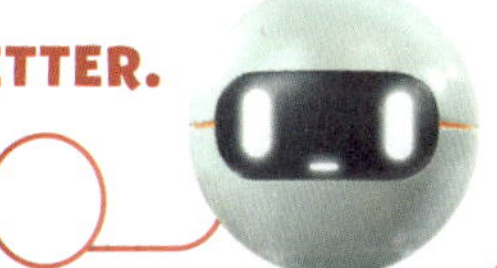

TIME TO LEARN ABOUT

MY SCHOOL

1. Read about Joana and her school. Complete the chart.

Hello! I'm Joana. I'm 11 years old and I'm at 5th grade at Santa Verona School. My school is 67 years old.

Go up the stairs and there are 10 classrooms and 4 toilets. Go down the stairs and there is a cafeteria. Go straight ahead the hall and there is a gym. Then turn left on the gym and there is a swimming pool. I love swimming and P.E. is my favorite subject.

dotshock/Shutterstock

Girl's name and age:	
Name and age of school:	
Girl's favorite place in school:	
Girl's favorite subject:	

2. Let's learn some directions.

SimeonVD/Shutterstock

THIS IS MY SCHOOL!

3. Write about your school and give directions of your favorite place.

____

____

____

____

4. Draw a map of your school.

Macrovector Art/Alamy/Fotoarena

UNIT

ARE YOU READY?

1. Listen and act out.  

Liz is helping Leo organize his daily routine.

Good morning, Leo! Get up. It's 7 o'clock. It's time to go to school.
Auuuugh! Good morning, mom!

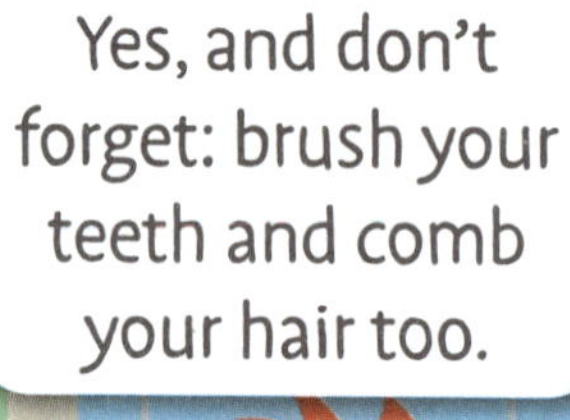

First, take...
I know, mom... take a shower, get dressed and have breakfast.

Yes, and don't forget: brush your teeth and comb your hair too.

Ilustrações: Marcos Mello/Arquivo da editora

It's 3:30 p.m. Leo is back from school.
Hi, mom! I'm here.
Hi, dear!
Oh, mom, I'm so tired.
So, rest a bit, Leo.
Thanks, mom!
But then, at 4:00 p.m....
I know... first do my homework, and then I can play and watch TV.
Super! You're a good boy.

FINDING OUT

2. Complete the blanks with words from the box.
Then listen and check your answers.  

A day in the life of a firefighter

special • equipment • physical • firefighter • lunch • training • prevention • fire station

Every day can be different, but a typical one can be like this...

Dora is a ____________. She loves her job.

Tyler Olson/Shutterstock

Joe Benning/Shutterstock

It's 7:45 a.m. Dora starts her day at the ____________.

Tyler Olson/Shutterstock

It's 8:15 a.m. It's time to check out the ____________.

MZeta/Shutterstock

It's 10:00 a.m. It's time for the firefighters to do ____________ activities!

Stephane Gautier/Alamy/Fotoarena

It's 12:00 o'clock. It's time to have ____________!

Other firefighters are at the fire station alert!

During lunch time the bell rings. Some firefighters rush to the fire truck. It's a road traffic collision with people trapped inside the cars.

At 1:00 p.m. it's time for ____________, doing business inspections and special programs.

At 3:00 p.m. it's time for ____________ and protection.

Kzenon/Shutterstock

At 7:00 p.m. it's time to write the reports or work on ____________ projects.

WORD WORK

3. Listen, stick and say.

At home, it's time to...
get up
take a shower
get dressed
comb the hair
brush the teeth
have breakfast
go to school
do homework

At school, it's time to...
open the book
close the book
sit down
stand up
be quiet, please

4. Circle eight actions. Write them under the pictures.

B	A	M	W	R	I	T	E	J	S	I	T
R	I	O	K	O	A	E	I	O	T	O	N
U	I	O	P	C	L	O	S	E	A	P	L
S	C	R	T	E	W	I	O	P	N	E	W
H	R	I	O	U	T	E	J	L	D	N	A
S	I	T	*	D	O	W	N	E	*	S	T
E	T	Y	M	H	I	O	P	O	U	Y	C
P	L	A	Y	J	K	L	O	U	P	S	H

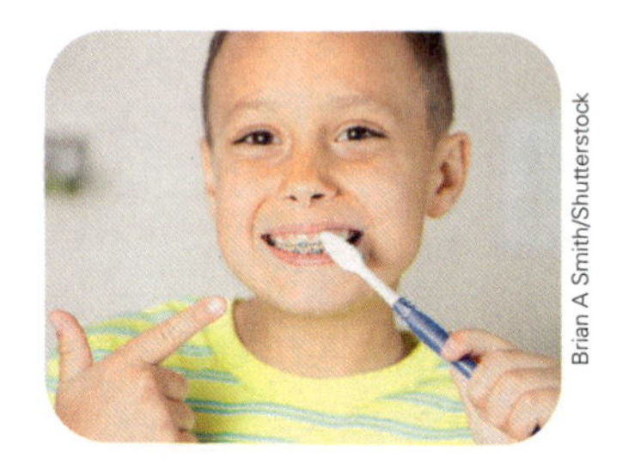
Brian A Smith/Shutterstock

a) ____________________
the teeth.

. moodboard/Alamy/Fotoarena

b) ____________________
now.

Photo_Concepts/Cultura RF/Getty Images

c) ____________________
here.

Pavel L Photo and Video/Shutterstock

d) ____________________
chess.

Zurijeta/Shutterstock

e) ____________________
the door.

stockfour/Shutterstock

f) ____________________
the door.

vectorfusionart/ Shutterstock

g) ____________________
the soccer match.

Syda Productions/ Shutterstock

h) ____________________
your name.

LISTENING AND ORAL PRACTICE

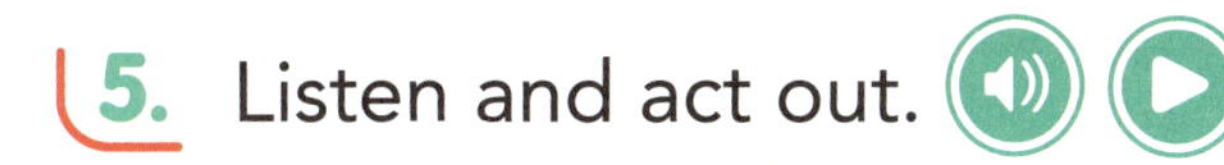

5. Listen and act out.

Mrs. Smith: Class... silence, please! Paul, stand up, can you come here and solve this addition on the board?

Paul: Yes, teacher! Two plus four equals six!

Mrs. Smith: It's correct! Thank you, Paul! Now, go sit down!

Paul: OK, teacher.

Mrs. Smith: Now, close your books. It's recess time.

Paul: Have a great time, Mrs. Smith!

Mrs. Smith: Thanks, Paul!

wavebreakmedia/Shutterstock

6. Listen to Bob and Lisa and check only the true information.

a) ◯ My day starts at 7 a.m. I go the bathroom and brush my teeth.

b) ◯ I have breakfast with my mom and sister. My dad leaves earlier.

c) ◯ I go to school by bus.

d) ◯ After I finish school, I go to the club.

e) ◯ I am crazy about dance.

f) ◯ I have dinner with my family at 7:30 p.m.

LANGUAGE ACTIVITIES

Telling time

What time is it?

05:00	It's five o'clock.	05:30	It's five thirty.
05:05	It's five-oh-five.	05:35	It's five thirty-five.
05:10	It's _______ ten.	05:40	It's five _______.
05:15	It's five fifteen.	05:45	It's five forty-five.
05:20	It's five twenty.	05:50	It's five fifty.
05:25	It's five _______.	05:55	It's five _______ .

Ilustrações: Ilustra Cartoon/Arquivo da editora

Say with Me!

From two to two past two.

What time is it?

Luiz Giope/Shutterstock

It's ten twenty a.m.

nevenm/Shutterstock

It's five-oh-five p.m.

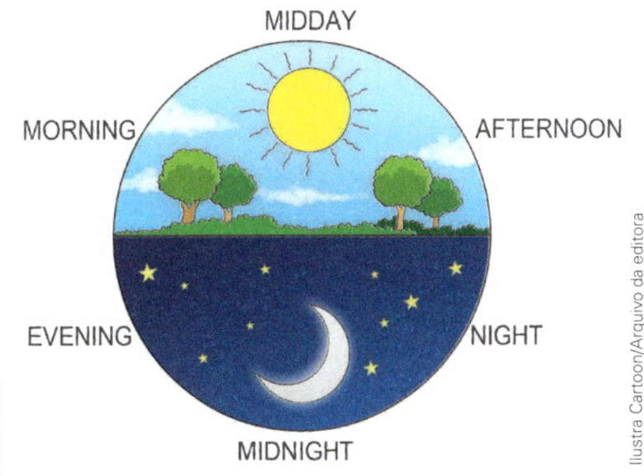

Ilustra Cartoon/Arquivo da editora

Netfalls Remy Musser/Shutterstock

midday/noon
12:00 p.m.

artshock/Shutterstock

midnight
12:00 a.m.

7. Complete the sentences based on your daily routine. 

a) In the morning ________________ at ________________ .

b) At noon I usually ________________ .

c) I go to school in the ________________ .

d) I usually do my homework at ________________ .

e) In the evening, I usually ________________ with my family at ________________ .

f) I watch TV at ________________ .

g) I usually go to sleep at ________________ .

8. Draw the clocks hands or write the hours and complete the sentences.

My daily routine

a) I get up at ______________.

b) I take a shower at ______________.

c) I have breakfast at ______________.

d) I go to school at ______________.

e) I have lunch at ______________.

f) I do my homework at ______________.

g) I play at ______________.

h) I watch TV at ______________.

i) I have dinner at ______________.

j) I go to bed at ______________.

Ilustrações: Sirayama/Arquivo da editora; Ilustra Cartoon/Arquivo da editora

9. Read and complete the dialog. 

sorry • teacher • time • is • school • wake up • o'clock

Emma: It's ________ to go to school, Charlie! ______________, son. It's seven ____________.

Charlie: ____________, mom. I'm not feeling well today.

Noah: Emma, please write a note to Charlie's ______________, Miss Miller. Tell her Charlie has a fever today. He ______ not going to ______________.

Emma: OK, Noah. Charlie, you stay in bed.

Charlie: Yes, mom.

10. Fill in the blanks with **am**, **is** or **are**. 

< > x

Dear Ms. Miller,

My name ______ Emma Davis. Charlie, Olivia and Will Davis ______ my children.

Will and Olivia ______ at school, but Charlie ______ at home with me. He ______ not feeling well today.

He ______ in bed resting now. He has a fever. Please send me his homework.

Thank you!

Yours sincerely,
Emma Davis

Estúdio Ornitorrinco/Arquivo da editora

Text 1

Time zone

As the Earth rotates on its axis, the Sun shines on only one part of the Earth at a time. While the sun shines where you live, it's nighttime somewhere else. When you're eating your breakfast cereal, children in Paris are finishing the school day and children in Moscow are eating dinner. Children in Bangkok are going to bed and children in Sydney, Australia, are getting up for the next day of school. [...]

Available at: https://easyscienceforkids.com/all-about-the-time-zone/. Accessed on: February 28, 2022.

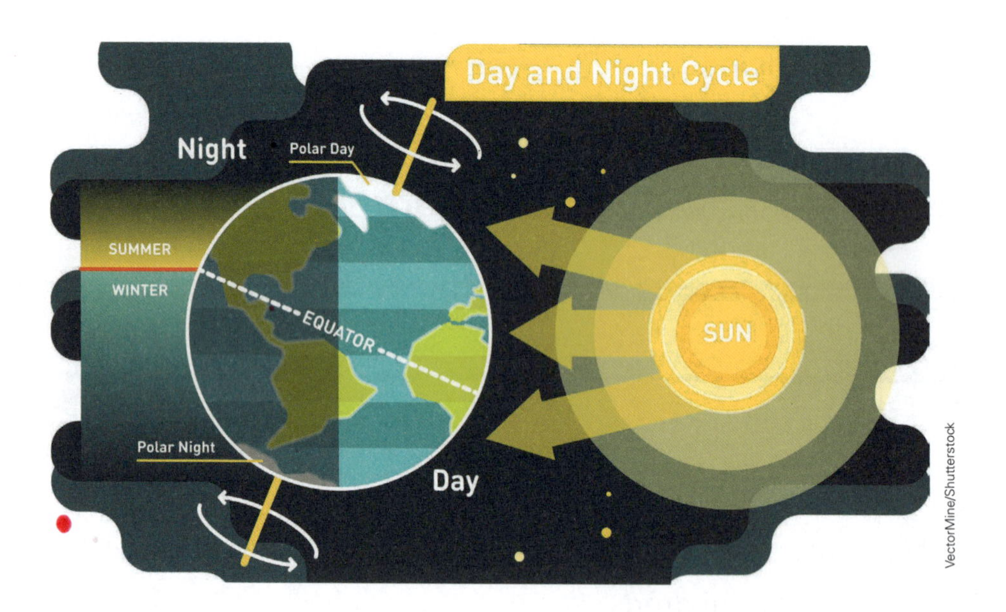

VectorMine/Shutterstock

11. Read the text and answer **T** (for true) or **F** (for false).  

a) ◯ The Sun shines on only one part of the Earth at a time.

b) ◯ When the sun shines where you live, it's nighttime somewhere else in the world.

c) ◯ While children in Bangkok are going to bed, children in Sydney are going to bed too.

d) ◯ The text mentions one country and four cities.

12. Look at the clocks. They show different times in the world. 

WHAT TIME IS IT IN...

a) New York? ____________________

b) Paris? ____________________

c) Moscow? ____________________

d) Beijing? ____________________

e) Sydney? ____________________

vtwinpixel/Shutterstock

Text 2

WHAT'S ON TV?

13. Read the TV schedule and circle.  

a) The text is a:
- TV schedule guide
- TV slogan

b) On Saturday morning the cartoon that starts at 6:00 is ...
- Kitty Explorer
- Bob the Centipede

c) What time can you watch Rainbow Power on TV?
- At 7 a.m.
- At 7:30 a.m.

d) You can watch George, the Flamingo on...
- Saturdays and Sundays.
- Fridays and Sundays.

CTN TV
CARTOON SCHEDULE
SATURDAY MORNING
6:00 – Bob the Centipede
6:30 – Bob the Centipede
7:00 – Kitty Explorer
7:30 – George the Flamingo
8:00 – Bunny Dream Team
8:30 – Lily and Rose Tales
SUNDAY MORNING
6:00 – Kitty Explorer
6:30 – Kitty Explorer
7:00 – My Dog Tommy
7:30 – Rainbow Power
8:00 – George the Flamingo
8:30 – George the Flamingo

Available on: <https://pbswisconsin.org/article/pbs-kids-fall-updates/>. Accessed on March 22, 2022.

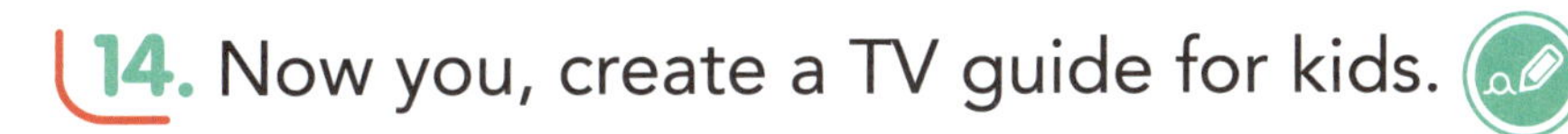

14. Now you, create a TV guide for kids.

LET'S SING!

Every day, every day!

Every day, every day!
What do you do every day?
I wake up in the morning
I wash my face
I brush my teeth
I comb my hair
I eat breakfast
and here I go... to school!
Byeeeeeeee!
Byeeeeeeeeeee!

Ilustrações: Ilustra Cartoon/Arquivo da editora

163 WB

15. Number the daily actions according to the song.

( ) Go to school
( ) Comb the hair
( ) Wake up
( ) Wash the face
( ) Eat breakfast
( ) Brush the teeth

16. Now you write the actions according to your daily routine.

____

____

____

____

____

____

GROWING UP

BE RESPONSIBLE AND PUNCTUAL!

17. Look at the cartoon and talk to your classmates. 

18. In pairs, write a dialog and act out.  

A: Good morning! Listen, the alarm clock is ringing!

B: Oh, please! Let me sleep!

A: It's time to get up! You're late for school!

___

___

___

___

– +

CHECK YOUR PROGRESS

AWESOME! 

GOOD JOB! 

I CAN DO BETTER. 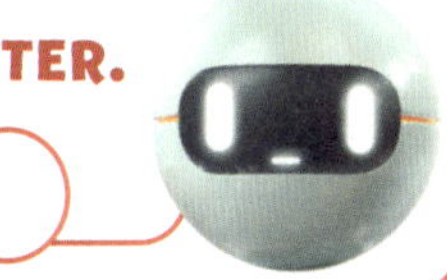

REVIEW

1. Unscramble and match.  

a) enniyt-htegi – ____________________ •

b) urenfote – ____________________ •

c) teelvw – ____________________ •

d) ffyit – ____________________ •

e) evsyent-eon – ____________________ •

f) irtyth-teher – ____________________ •

• 33

• 98

• 50

• 71

• 14

• 12

2. Read and complete the 5th grade school schedule.  

Break time is at 9:30. Science classes are on Mondays and Wednesdays. Art classes are on Tuesdays and Fridays. P. E. is on Tuesdays and Fridays at 9:50. Music is on Tuesdays at 8:40 and Wednesdays at 10:40.

5TH GRADE

Time	M_____day	T_____day	We_____day	T_____day	F_____ay
7:00	Math		Language Arts	History	Robotics
7:50	Math	Math	Language Arts	Language Arts	Language Arts
8:40	Language Arts		Geography	Robotics	History
9:30		Recess	Recess	Recess	
9:50	Science		Math	Math	
10:40	Science	Language Arts		Math	Math
11:30 – 12:20	History	Language Arts	Science	Geography	

3. Write the sentences in the correct speech bubbles. 

John, stand up! • Melissa, silence, please!
Billy, sit down here, please! • Caroline, pay attention!

Ilustrações: Ilustra Cartoon/Arquivo da editora

4. Write the time in full. 

a) 6:00 p. m. – ______

b) 7:30 a. m. – ______

c) 9:40 p. m. – ______

d) 11:15 a. m. – ______

e) 12:00 p. m. – ______

UNIT

3 CAN YOU PLAY THE DRUMS?

1. Listen and act out.  

Ilustrações: Marcos Mello/Arquivo da editora

You can do this, too! I can help you!
Yes, please do, grandpa!
First, sit straight, please.
OK, grandpa!
I'm ready!
Hold the drumsticks correctly...
Now, hands crossed. Right hand, right foot...
Great job, Leo!
First beat. Count 1, 1, 2! 1, 1, 2!
1, 1, 2! 1, 1, 2! Whoopiee! I can! I can!
Grandpa, you're the best!
Please, Leo! No need to play so loud!

FINDING OUT

2. Look at the pictures and make an **X**. Then listen and check your answer.

They're about  sports.  games.  hobbies.

YanLev/Shutterstock

George Rudy/Shutterstock

AnaWhite/Shutterstock

Iakov Filimonov/Shutterstock

wavebreakmedia/Shutterstock

Fotokostic/Shutterstock

Serhii Bobyk/Shutterstock

Lordn/Shutterstock

antoniodiaz/Shutterstock

Sklo Studio/Shutterstock

sirtravelalot/Shutterstock

Hatchapong Palurtchaivong/Shutterstock

3. Match the activities below to the pictures in activity 2. 

a) writing
b) playing soccer
c) painting
d) photography
e) playing an instrument
f) watching movies
g) playing tennis
h) listening to music
i) swimming
j) reading books
k) cooking
l) gardening

4. Ask a classmate: "What's your favorite hobby?". 

5. Listen, stick and say.

Can you...?

draw

paint

play the bass

act

dance

play the drums

sing

play the guitar

sculpt

6. Match and write.  

Alinne Volpato/Acervo da fotógrafa

Kevin Mazur/Getty Images

Kevin Mazur/Getty Images

Matthew Stockman/Getty Images

Ron Adar/Shutterstock

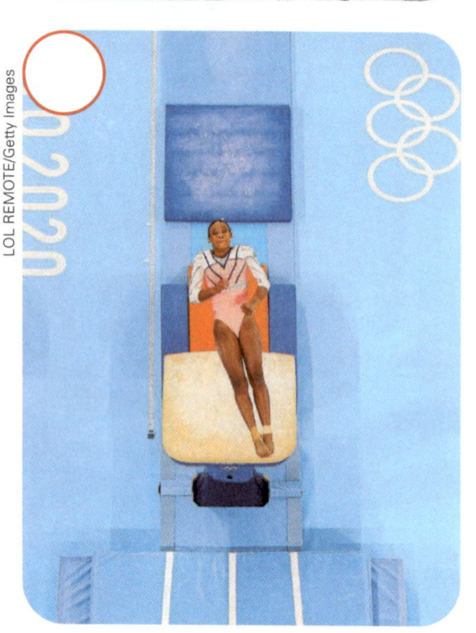
LOL REMOTE/Getty Images

a) Luiz Fernando Rego can dance ballet. ◯ can sing and act.

b) Olivia Rodrigo ______. ◯ can jump in the air.

c) OSGEMEOS ______. ◯ can play tennis.

d) Rafael Nadal ______. ◯ can dance ballet.

e) Daniel Radcliffe ______. ◯ can spray paint graffiti.

f) Rebeca Andrade ______. ◯ can act.

7. Make an X.

How are you feeling today?

Today, I'm ______________________.

Feelings

8. Circle the words and complete.  

A	W	Y	U	C	J	R	S	A	D
N	F	K	J	X	T	Y	O	S	D
G	G	L	Z	T	I	R	E	D	V
R	N	M	B	Z	Q	T	U	C	B
Y	A	S	X	H	M	Y	I	V	O
A	F	H	A	P	P	Y	G	D	R
F	C	U	S	Z	X	N	R	Q	E
G	Y	J	K	M	W	A	V	Z	D

C

Ilustrações: Ilustra Cartoon/Arquivo da editora

a) My brother is ______________________.

b) Your friend is ______________________.

c) The girl is ______________________.

d) My brother is ______________________.

e) The girl is ______________________.

LISTENING AND ORAL PRACTICE

9. Listen and check **can** or **can't**.  

	HELEN	ROBERT	MARK	SUSAN	MILLIE
CAN					
CAN'T					

Ilustra Cartoon/Arquivo da editora

10. Listen and number the pictures.  

How are you feeling today?

I'm happy. And you? ______________________

AmazeinDesign/Shutterstock

sylv1rob1/Shutterstock

Emily ◯

Nikolas_jkd/Shutterstock

Ellen ◯

Jihan Nafiaa Zahri/Shutterstock

Emmy ◯

11. Listen about things Nathalie and Gabriel **can** and **can't** do.

Igor Bulgarin/Shutterstock

Shoji Fujita/Digital Vision/Getty Images

	PLAY SOCCER	SING	DANCE	PLAY VOLLEYBALL	PLAY BASEBALL
NATHALIE					
GABRIEL					

12. Complete the sentences based on the information from activity 11.

a) Gabriel can ______________________________.

b) Gabriel can't ______________________________.

c) Nathalie can ______________________________.

d) Nathalie can't ______________________________.

LANGUAGE ACTIVITIES

Opposites

Good_Stock/Shutterstock

happy   sad

13. Complete the sentences with the words from the box. 

new • short • thin • pretty • big

a) One of the panda bears is fat. The other panda is ______________.

Jordi Fernandez Ventura/Shutterstock

b) The elephant is ______________.
The mouse is small.

GraphicsRF.com/Shutterstock

c) Look at the shoes! One is ______________ and the other is old.

TINA NIZOVA/Shutterstock

d) One of the girls is ______________.
The other girl is ugly.

TINA NIZOVA/Shutterstock

e) The giraffe is tall. The tiger is ______________.

Good_Stock/Shutterstock

READ AND WRITE

Text

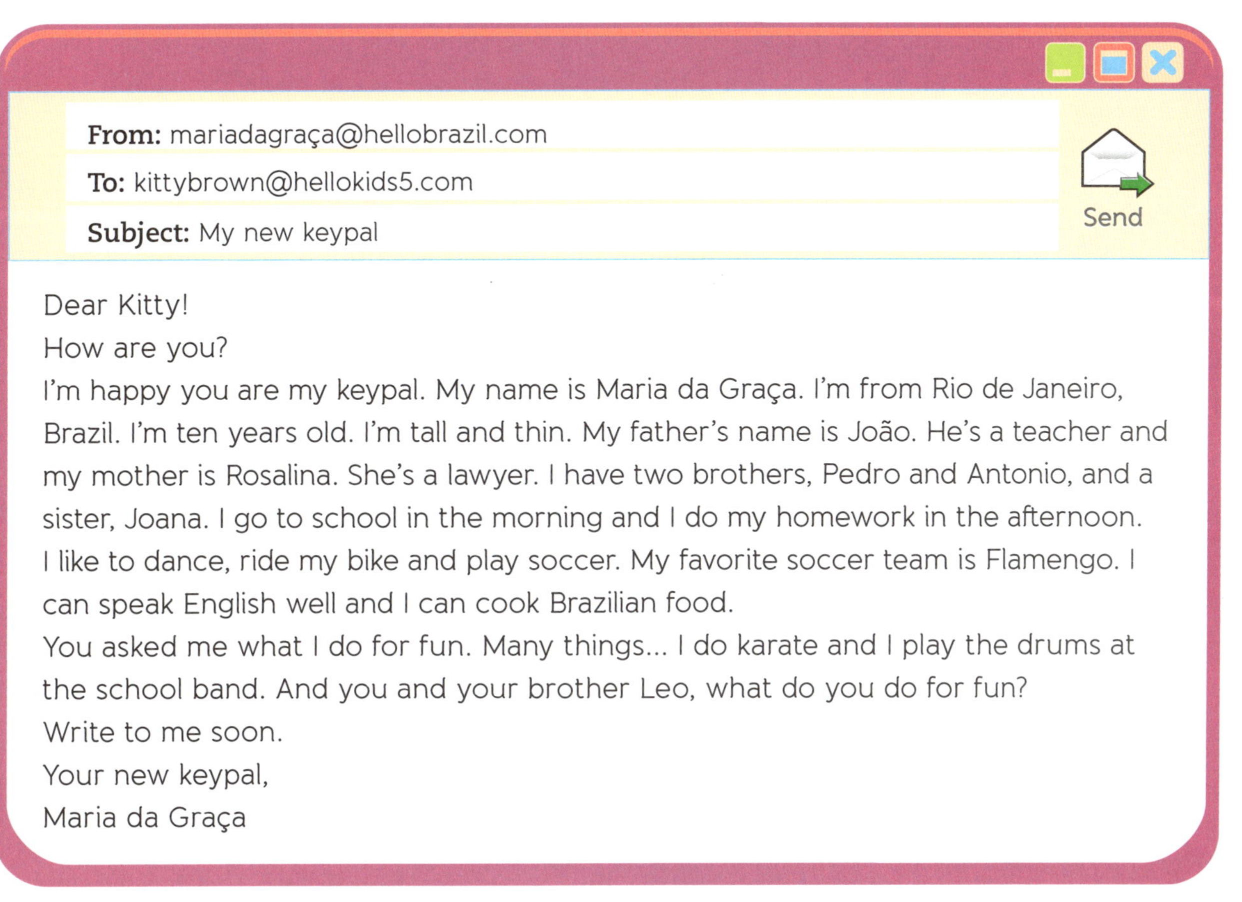

From: mariadagraça@hellobrazil.com

To: kittybrown@hellokids5.com

Subject: My new keypal

Send

Dear Kitty!

How are you?

I'm happy you are my keypal. My name is Maria da Graça. I'm from Rio de Janeiro, Brazil. I'm ten years old. I'm tall and thin. My father's name is João. He's a teacher and my mother is Rosalina. She's a lawyer. I have two brothers, Pedro and Antonio, and a sister, Joana. I go to school in the morning and I do my homework in the afternoon. I like to dance, ride my bike and play soccer. My favorite soccer team is Flamengo. I can speak English well and I can cook Brazilian food.

You asked me what I do for fun. Many things... I do karate and I play the drums at the school band. And you and your brother Leo, what do you do for fun?

Write to me soon.

Your new keypal,

Maria da Graça

14. Write **T** for true or **F** for false. 

a) Maria is fat and short.

b) She has two brothers and three sisters.

c) Maria goes to school in the morning.

d) She likes to sing and cook.

e) Maria can speak English very well.

15. Write a message to a keypal from another country. 

LET'S SING!

How do you feel today?

I feel tired.
I feel bored.
I feel sad.
I feel terrible today,
but now I'm feeling OK!

I feel happy.
I feel loved.
I feel great.
I feel hopeful today,
now, it's a happy, happy day,
hooray, hooray, hooray!

Ilustra Cartoon/Arquivo da editora

16. Unscramble the words and draw emoticons.

DIRTE	OREBD	DAS	BELRRIET
______	______	______	______

PPHAY	DEVOL	TAGRE	LFUEOPH
______	______	______	______

165 WB

Say with Me!

Happy for a minute, sad for a second,
heart eyes, smiling face, blowing a
kiss, emojis are cool!

GROWING UP

BE KIND, POLITE AND HAPPY.

17. Look at the picture and talk to your classmates. 

18. In groups, make cards using emojis to represent: Be on time, and ready to learn. Respect when others are speaking. Be polite. Say "please" and "thank you". Raise your hand for permission to speak.

19. Break the code.

CHECK YOUR PROGRESS
AWESOME!
GOOD JOB!
I CAN DO BETTER.

TIME TO LEARN ABOUT

LET'S DANCE!

1. Look at the picture, read the text and answer.

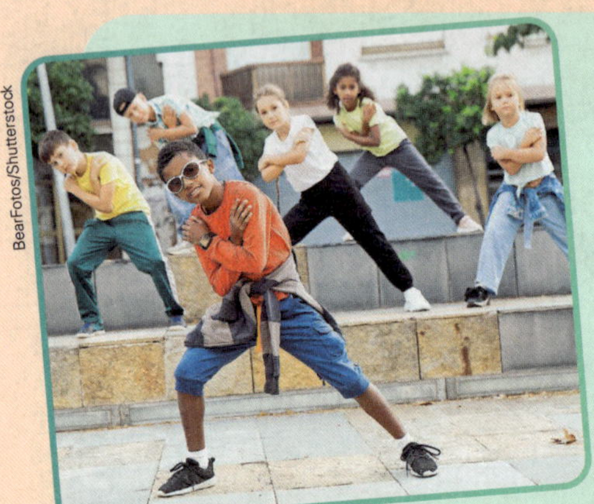
BearFotos/Shutterstock

Break dancing

Break dancing, also called breaking and B-boying, energetic form of dance, fashioned and popularized by African Americans and Latinos, that includes stylized footwork and athletic moves such as back spins or head spins. Break dancing originated in New York City during the late 1960s and early '70s, incorporating moves from a variety of sources, including martial arts and gymnastics. [...]

It is also associated with a particular style of dress that includes baggy pants or sweat suits, baseball caps worn sideways or backward, and sneakers (required because of the dangerous nature of many of the moves). [...] The term break refers to the particular rhythms and sounds produced by deejays by mixing sounds from records to produce a continuous dancing beat.

Extracted from: https://www.britannica.com/art/break-dance.
Accessed on: Mar. 17, 2022.

a) Are there any other names for break dancing?

( ) Breaking and B-boying.

( ) Fighting martial arts.

b) Who popularized break dancing?

( ) African Americans and Latinos.

( ) Brazilians and Latinos.

c) Where is break dancing originally from?

- ◯ London, England.
- ◯ New York, U.S.A.

d) What kind of clothes and accessories do break dancers wear?

- ◯ Baggy pants or sweat suits, baseball caps, and sneakers.
- ◯ Kung Fu pants, baseball caps, and shoes.

2. Look at these break dance moves. Are they difficult?

Ilustrações: Ilustra Cartoon/Arquivo da editora

WE LIKE DANCING!

3. In groups, let's participate on a dance contest.

GARUDA PROJECT/Shutterstock

UNIT

4 THE E-GENERATION

1. Listen and act out.  

The Brown family is at home. Everybody is on the Internet.
Hi, Fido! Do you want to go outside?

Leo, it's time to take Fido for a walk.

Sorry, mom! I'm doing my homework.

Ilustrações: Marcos Mello/Arquivo da editora

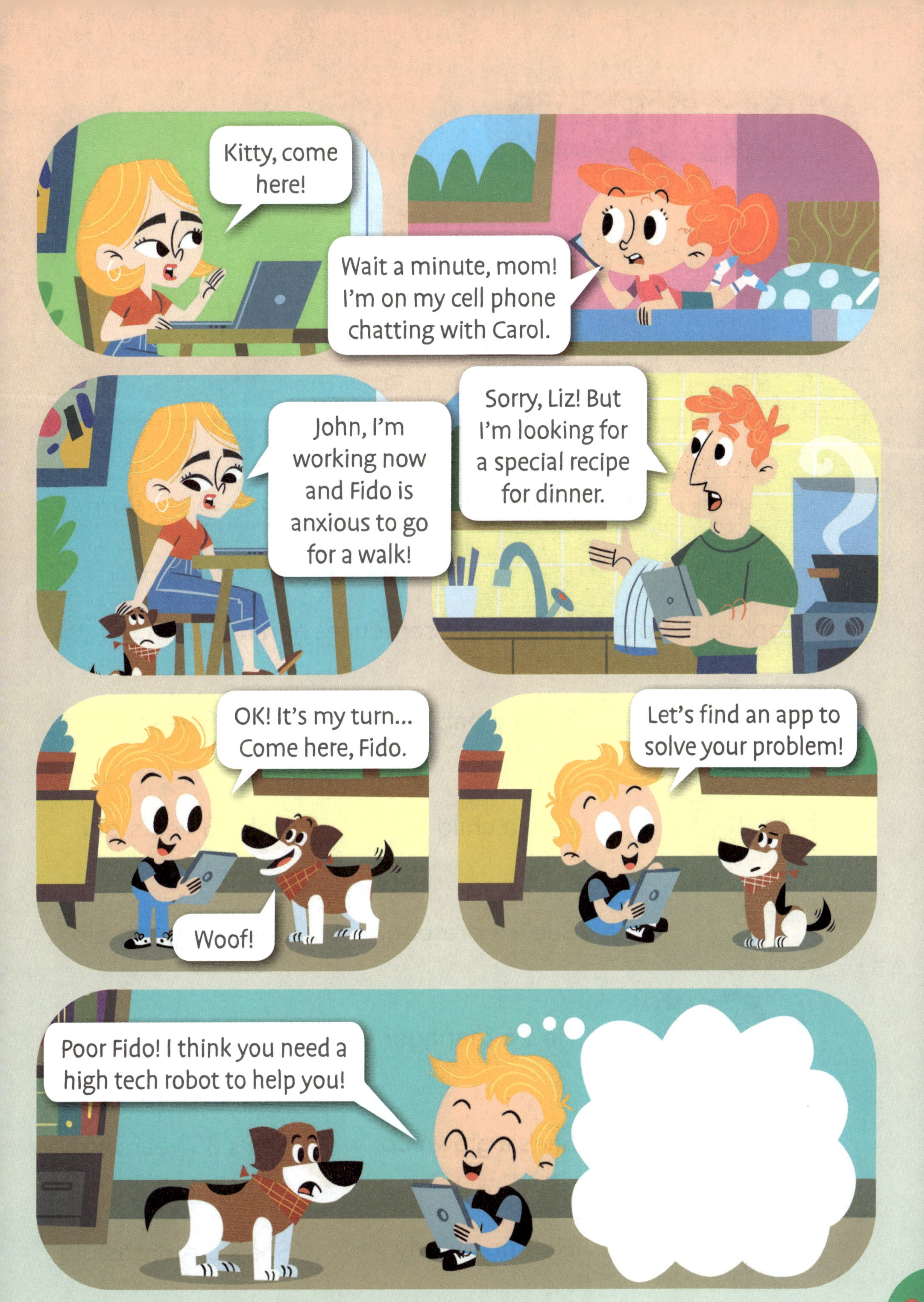
Kitty, come here!
Wait a minute, mom! I'm on my cell phone chatting with Carol.
John, I'm working now and Fido is anxious to go for a walk!
Sorry, Liz! But I'm looking for a special recipe for dinner.
OK! It's my turn... Come here, Fido.
Woof!
Let's find an app to solve your problem!
Poor Fido! I think you need a high tech robot to help you!

FINDING OUT

This is life!

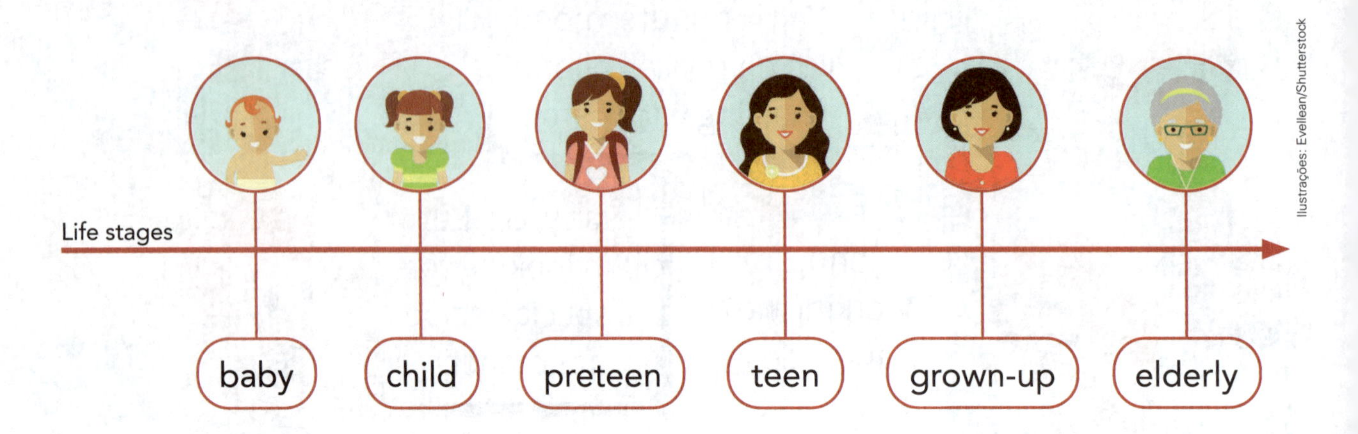

Ilustrações: Evellean/Shutterstock

2. Look at the pictures, read the sentences and match them. 

Monkey Business Images/Shutterstock

Kostiantyn Ablazov/Shutterstock

ViDI Studio/Shutterstock

Billion Photos/Shutterstock

Bernardo Emanuelle/Shutterstock

Roman Samborskyi/Shutterstock

1 She's a baby.	( ) He's 15 years old.
2 He's a child.	( ) He's 73 years old.
3 She's a preteen.	( ) She's 11 years old.
4 He's a teenager.	( ) He's 7 years old.
5 She's a grown-up.	( ) She's 35 years old.
6 He's an elderly.	( ) She's 5 months old.

3. Listen, stick and say.

What do you do when you are...?

a baby • a child • a preteen • a teen • a grown-up • an elderly

sleep

draw

cry

play app games

share photos and videos

go to parties

listen to music

work

pay bills

drive a car

do the homework

chat with friends on the cell phone

4. Write six actions using these letters. Match the actions to the pictures.

S C R I Y L P V W D A E N

a) ___ ___ Y

b) ___ ___ ___ V ___

c) ___ L ___ ___

d) ___ A ___ ___ ___

e) ___ ___ E ___ ___

f) D ___ ___ ___

wavebreakmedia/Shutterstock

Maja Marjanovic/Shutterstock

michaeljung/Shutterstock

Hung Chung Chih/Shutterstock

Robert Kneschke/Shutterstock

Natee K Jindakum/Shutterstock

LISTENING AND ORAL PRACTICE

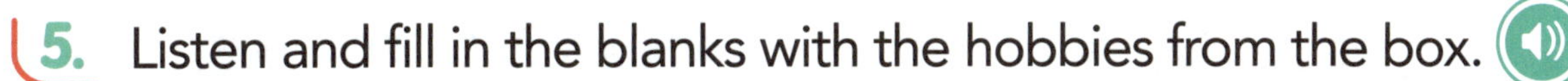

5. Listen and fill in the blanks with the hobbies from the box.  

skateboarding • watch TV series • cricket • the guitar • robotics • blogging • computer games • chat with friends

a) My hobbies are ____________ and ____________. I love building robots at school.

b) I like to play __________ and ________________. I'm good at Minecraft.

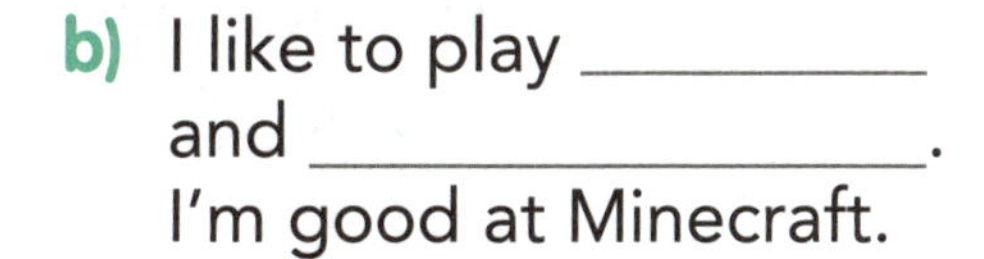

Ashley, 9
Sergey and Marina Pyataev/Shutterstock

Joe, 10
Anton Albert/Shutterstock

c) My hobbies are playing __________ and __________. I have a blog about video game preferences.

d) My favorite hobbies? I like to ________________ and ________________ on my cell phone.

Matt, 8
VALUA VITALY/Shutterstock

Emily, 9
Alex Vog/Shutterstock

6. Listen and write **Yes** or **No**.  

a) 
Prostock-studio/Shutterstock

b) 
Andrey Arkusha/Shutterstock

c) 
yongtick/Shutterstock

d) 
Prostock-studio/Shutterstock

7. Listen and act out.

Ilustrações: Marcos Mello/Arquivo da editora

LANGUAGE ACTIVITIES

Verb to be

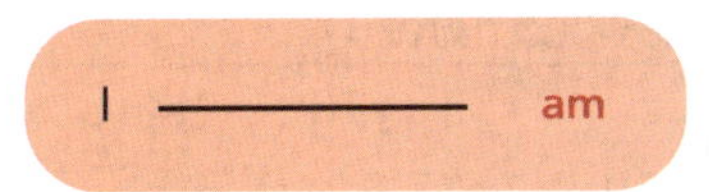

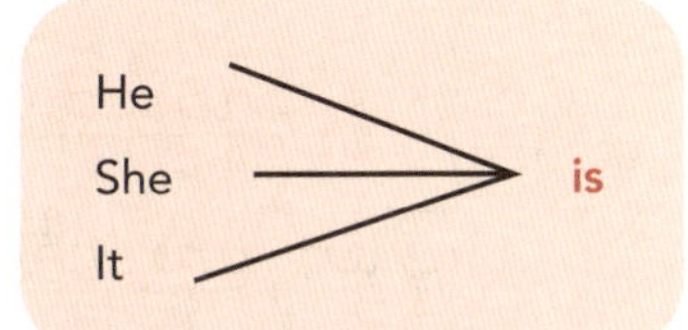

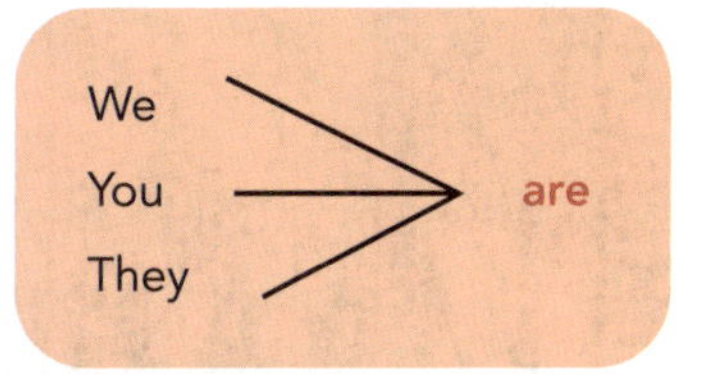

Affirmative form	Interrogative form	Negative form
He is my friend. They are in the classroom.	Is he my friend? Are they in the classroom?	He is not (isn't) my friend. They are not (aren't) in the classroom.

8. Write the correct form of the verb **to be**. 

a) ______________ she sad?

No, she ______________. She ______________ tired.

b) ______________ he seven years old?

No, he ______________. He ______________ an elderly person. He ______________ seventy years old.

c) ______________ they angry?

No, they ______________. They ______________ happy.

AmazeinDesign/Shutterstock

9. Look at the pictures, unscramble the questions and answer them.

JGA/Shutterstock

a) they / are / teenagers / ?

Are they teenagers?

No, they are not (aren't).

They are children.

Anatoliy Karlyuk/Shutterstock

b) he / child / is / a / ?

___

___

___

Roman Samborskyi/Shutterstock

c) grown-up / is / a / she / ?

___

___

___

wavebreakmedia/Shutterstock

d) elderly / are / they / ?

___

___

___

10. Complete the conversations. 

it's • I am (2) • is • are • we • they • are you (2)

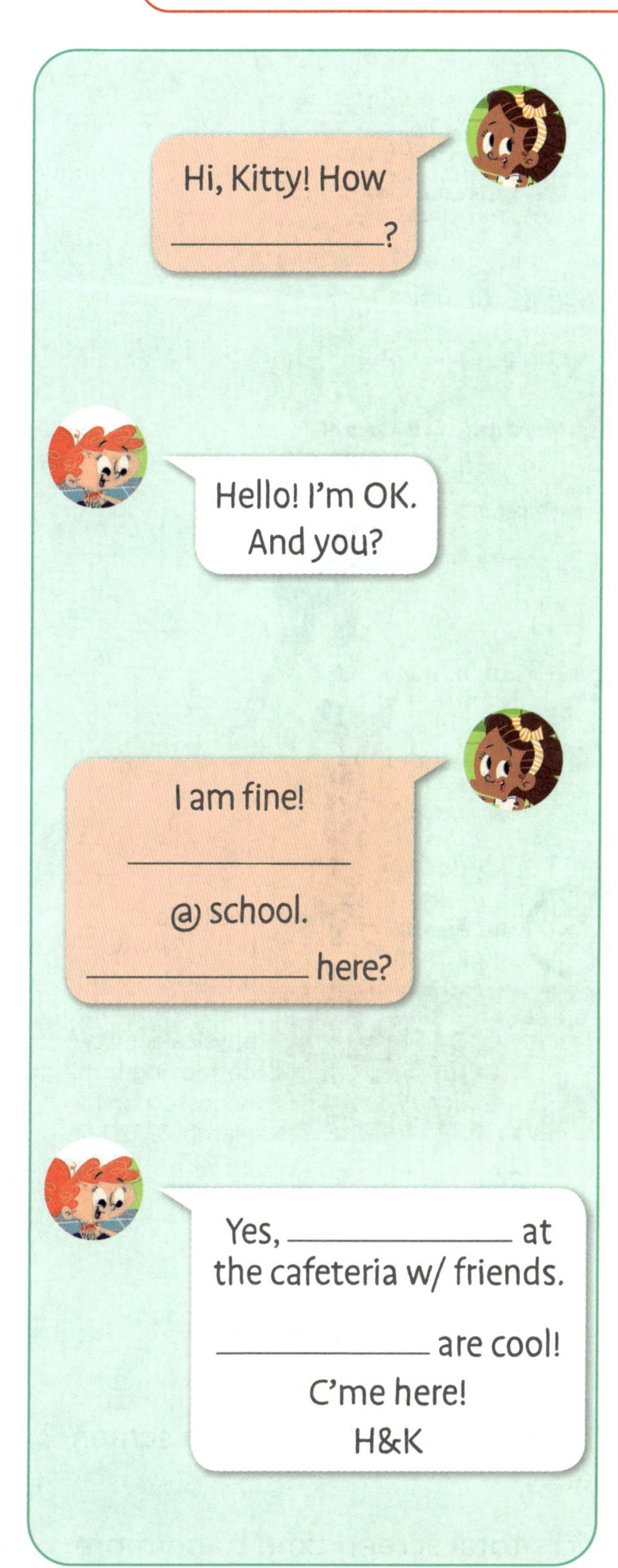

Hi, Kitty! How ___________?
Hello! I'm OK. And you?
I am fine! ___________ @ school. ___________ here?
Yes, ___________ at the cafeteria w/ friends. ___________ are cool! C'me here! H&K

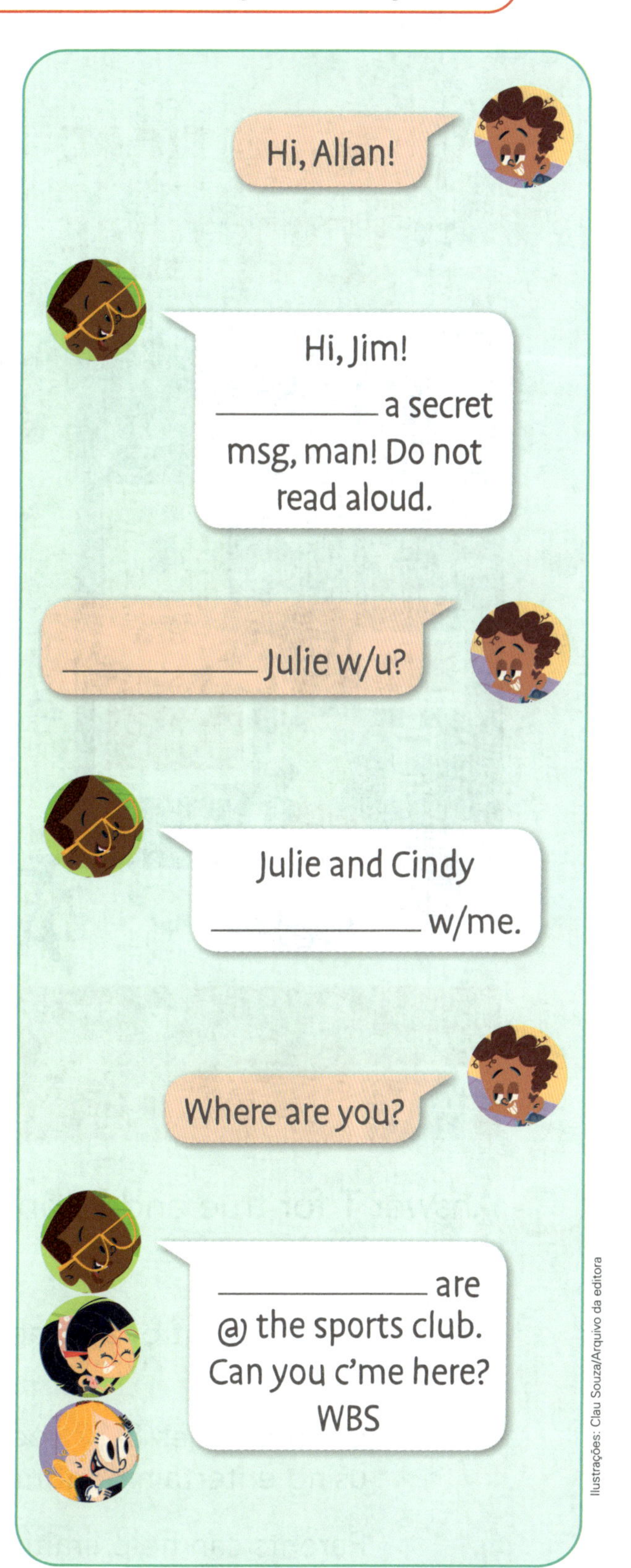

Hi, Allan!
Hi, Jim! ___________ a secret msg, man! Do not read aloud.
___________ Julie w/u?
Julie and Cindy ___________ w/me.
Where are you?
___________ are @ the sports club. Can you c'me here? WBS

Ilustrações: Clau Souza/Arquivo da editora

READ AND WRITE

Text 1

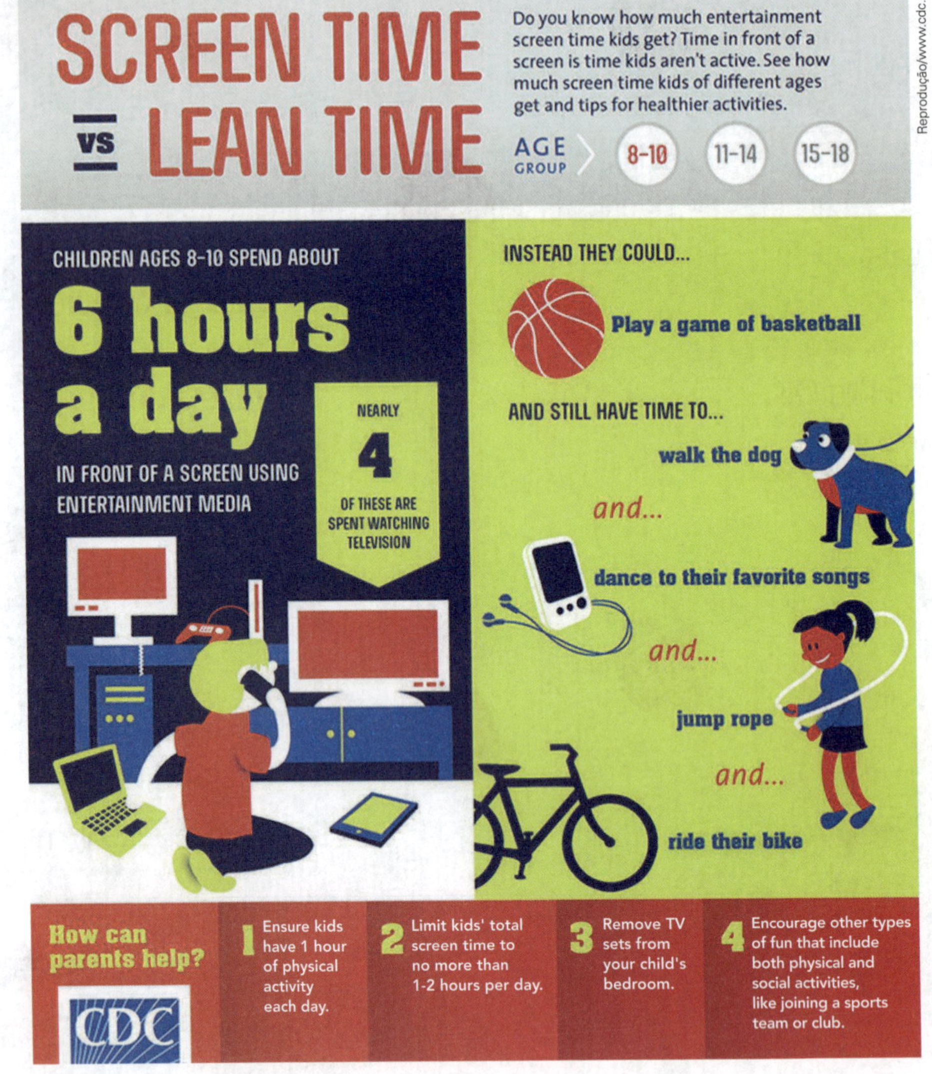

Available at: https://www.cdc.gov/healthyschools/physicalactivity/getmoving.htm. Accessed on: March 29, 2022.

11. Answer **T** for true and **F** for false.

a) ◯ Time in front of a screen is time kids aren't active.

b) ◯ Children ages 8-10 spend 8 hours a day in front of a screen using entertainment media.

c) ◯ Parents can help limiting kid's total screen time to no more than 6-8 hours per day.

Text 2

Inspiring kids

These days people say kids are in front of their computers, tablets or cell phones, playing games all day. But there are plenty of children who are spending their spare time making a difference in the lives of others in their communities. Look at an example:

Jaylen Arnold

Dia Dipasupil/Getty Images

Jaylen Arnold is a young boy who has Tourette's syndrome, a neurological disorder that causes motor and vocal tics. Because of his illness he endured [...] bullying at school [...]. Instead, Arnold decided to start a campaign called Jaylen's Challenge to stop school bullying. Through the Jaylen's Challenge website he sells anti-bullying wristbands and accepts donations for his cause [...] His efforts have inspired both students and school staff around the country to take a stand against school bullying.

Available at: www.beliefnet.com/inspiration/most-inspiring-of-the-month/september/miom-september.aspx?p=8#k4dhoFoy1aTTQbha.99. Accessed on: March 1, 2022.

12. Write **T** (True) or **F** (False).

a) ◯ There are kids who are spending their spare time making a difference in the lives of others.

b) ◯ People say adults play video games all day.

c) ◯ Jaylen Arnold is a young doctor.

d) ◯ Arnold decided to start a campaign to stop school bullying.

13. Think about an ideia to make a difference.  

Draw a wristband and write a sentence in it for your campaign.

LET'S SING!

Thumb generation

( ) I'm portable, I'm touchable,
I'm connected to the Internet!
I'm portable, I'm touchable,
I'm connected to the Internet!
I'm the thumb generation! (2 ×)

( ) I'm a teenager
I'm connected to the Internet
All the time, all the time!

( ) I play games,
I text messages, many messages.
All the time, all the time!

( ) I'm a teenager
I listen to music in my cell phone
All the time, all the time!

( ) I'm a teenager
I post pictures and make selfies
All the time, all the time!

14. Number the stanzas in order. 

167 WB

Say with Me!

I'm Kiddie5. Keep it in your mind.
I'm a high-tech machine but always
so kind, so kind!

15. Look at the picture and talk to your classmates. 

Monkey Business Images/Shutterstock

16. Create a T-shirt drawing.  

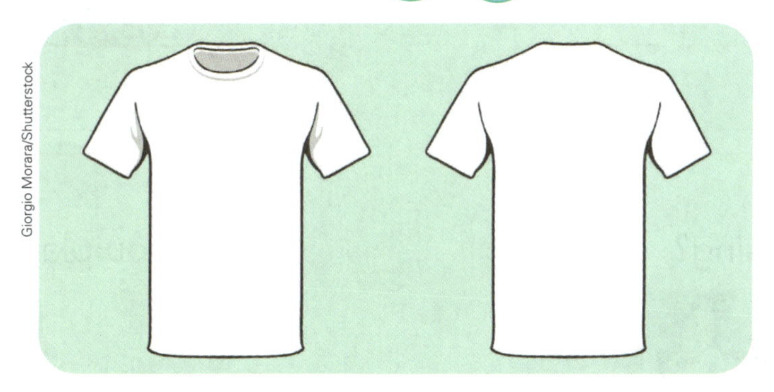
Giorgio Morara/Shutterstock

CHECK YOUR PROGRESS

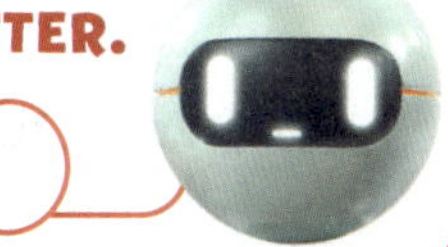

REVIEW

1. Read and circle the opposite.  

a)	**fat**	thin	tall	old
b)	**big**	cute	sun	small
c)	**happy**	sun	sad	old
d)	**tall**	short	small	sad
e)	**kind**	happy	rude	tall
f)	**old**	sad	ugly	new
g)	**ugly**	pretty	fat	short
h)	**angry**	bored	calm	surprised

2. Read and answer.  

a) Can you swim?

Studio Romantic/Shutterstock

____

b) Can you cook?

Catalin Petolea/Shutterstock

____

c) Can you sing?

Estrada Anton/Shutterstock

____

d) Can you play the piano?

hanapon1002/Shutterstock

____

Now you:

What can you do? ______________________________

3. Complete according to the pictures. 

cry • work • drive a car • chat on the Internet • play • sleep • pay lots of bills • play with friends • go to parties • do your homework

a) When you're a baby, you

_______________, _______________

and _______________________________.

pixelheadphoto digitalskillet/Shutterstock

b) When you're a child, you

____

and _______________________________.

ESB Professional/Shutterstock

c) When you're a teenager, you

____

and _______________________________.

Torgado/Shutterstock

d) When you're a grown-up, you

_______________, _______________

and _______________________________.

wong yu liang/Shutterstock

UNIT

5 NATURE AND PICNIC

1. Listen and act out.  

In the Botanical Garden
Hurray!
Boys and girls... Today is "the day". Let's have a class in the Botanical Garden and then have a picnic!

It's spring! Look at the different species of flowers, birds and insects in this season and take notes.

Marcos Mello/Arquivo da editora

Look at these ants!
Amazing! They are all in line!
OK, kids! It's picnic time!
And I have a tuna sandwich and orange juice.
I have some spinach pie and some grapes.
I have a chicken wrap and a delicious carrot cake.
Very good, kids! Only healthy food!
By the way, where is the apple juice?
Oh, it's here!

FINDING OUT

2. Look at the pictures and make an **X**. 

Rawpixel.com/Shutterstock

A Family's Day Picnic

Artepics/Alamy/Fotoarena/Coleção particular

English: "A Picnic, 1857" (oil on canvas). Date: 1857, author: Henry Nelson O'Neil.

a) ◯ Picture 2 was painted by Henry Nelson O'Neil.

b) ◯ Picture 2 was painted in 1957.

c) ◯ Picture 1 is about a Family's Day picnic.

d) ◯ In Pictures 1 and 2 we can see families.

3. In pairs, complete the chart.

	Picture 1	Picture 2
Number of people	There are ______ people in this picture.	There are ______ people in this picture.
Food and drink	Probably fruits, ______.	Probably meat, ______.

4. Answer: what kind of food would you take to a picnic?

____

5. Listen, stick and say.

Having fun in a picnic!

Picnic food

6. Wordsearch. Guess the words! 

a) You eat with a F__________, a __________ and a S__________N.

b) You use it to clean your mouth. N__________

c) You put stuff inside it to go to a picnic. P__________C __________T

d) You use it to drink water, juice etc. __________A__________

e) It's a fruit. It's green, red, big, sweet and heavy. W__________N

f) You drink it. It's made of fruits. J__________

g) You put it on the table to have dinner or lunch.

T__________EC__________H

h) You put food on it to eat. __________E

P	C	V	B	W	N	A	P	K	I	N	S	J	C	E	R	Y	Z
A	P	I	C	N	I	C	*	B	A	S	K	E	T	J	M	K	I
B	C	D	S	K	E	R	W	E	C	U	F	I	C	U	N	N	T
P	L	A	T	E	D	P	O	O	B	S	E	F	W	I	I	I	S
E	P	S	O	O	N	S	T	E	R	R	G	D	F	C	B	F	M
W	Q	E	X	F	G	P	O	R	K	L	H	T	A	E	I	E	P
A	S	F	A	S	D	O	W	A	R	T	W	E	G	N	H	Y	O
Z	F	O	R	K	M	O	E	Y	H	U	N	Y	Q	E	L	Y	J
Q	W	F	S	I	F	N	A	T	A	B	L	E	C	L	O	T	H
G	L	A	S	S	T	Z	Y	W	A	T	E	R	M	E	L	O	N

7. Listen, stick and say.

The seasons of the year are...

spring | summer | fall | winter

8. Read and answer.

a) What's your favorite season?

My favorite season is ______________________________ .

b) What's the season in Brazil now? ______________________________ .

9. Read and make an **X**.

a) In this season, there are lots of flowers.

spring ◯ winter ◯ fall ◯ summer ◯

b) It is very hot in this season.

spring ◯ winter ◯ fall ◯ summer ◯

c) This is the season of tree leaves falling.

spring ◯ winter ◯ fall ◯ summer ◯

d) It's very cold in this season.

spring ◯ winter ◯ fall ◯ summer ◯

LISTENING AND ORAL PRACTICE

10. Listen to the interview and write.  

a)

Alexander Raths/Shutterstock

Character: ______________________

Season: ______________________

____

b)

Sergio Stakhnyk/Shutterstock

Character: ______________________

Season: ______________________

____

c)

winyuu/Shutterstock

Character: ______________________

Season: ______________________

____

d)

Smit/Shutterstock

Character: ______________________

Season: ______________________

____

LANGUAGE ACTIVITIES

11. Read and complete.  

a) 
illustrissima/Shutterstock

I ________ two brothers.

b) 
Monkey Business Images/Shutterstock

They ________ a big car.

c) 
EllenSmile/Shutterstock

She ________ a new picnic basket.

To have (Present tense)	
I	have
You	
He	has
She	
It	
We	have
You	
They	

12. Complete with **has** or **have**. 

a) 
Darren Baker/Shutterstock

Lucy ________ a lot of apples.

b) 
Norb_KM/Shutterstock

I ________ a new cell phone.

c) 
Dragon Images/Shutterstock

They ________ a lovely family.

d) 
Chonlawut/Shutterstock

The boy ________ a cute dog.

Demonstrative pronouns

Singular	Plural
this → that	these → those

13. Look at the pictures and complete.

a 
________ bird is green.

b 
________ bird is blue.

c 
________ flowers are red.

d 
________ flowers are yellow.

14. Complete the gaps with this, that, these, those. 

a 
________ ant is red.

b 
________ ants are brown.

c 
________ ant is big.

d 
________ ants are hungry.

Oh, no... my cake!

Summer Picnic
PACKING LIST

Netrun78/Shutterstock

The Perfect Picnic

- [ ] Picnic Basket
- [ ] Ice packs
- [ ] Plastic utensils
- [ ] Napkins / paper towel
- [ ] Water
- [ ] Paper plates and cups
- [ ] Snacks: chips
- [ ] Fresh fruit
- [ ] Sandwiches
- [ ] Juice boxes
- [ ] Bug spray
- [ ] Sunscreen
- [ ] Scout the perfect location
- [ ] Picnic blanket
- [ ] Outdoor games
- [ ] Wireless speaker for music
- [ ] Create a playlist
- [ ] Camera
- [ ] Plastic containers for leftovers
- [ ] Garbage bag

Available at: https://sunnysweetdays.com/picnic-packing-list.
Accessed on: March 28, 2022.

15. Write **T** (True) or **F** (False). 

a) ◯ The text is a picnic checklist.

b) ◯ Outdoor games are on the list.

c) ◯ There are five items for food and drinks on the list.

d) ◯ Cameras, tablets and wireless speakers are items on the picnic list.

16. Go to the list and make an **X** in your "must have" items for a picnic.

LET'S SING!

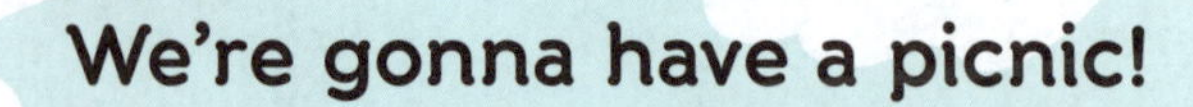

We're gonna have a picnic!

What a beautiful day!
We're gonna have a picnic.
What do you wanna eat?
Apples, cake, cookies,
juice and sandwiches.
Salad, chicken, cheese,
lemonade, ice cream.
Lots of food! Lots of food! (2×)
That's all we need for a picnic!

BNP Design Studio/Shutterstock

17. Write a picnic list with your five favorite kinds of food. Then draw them.  

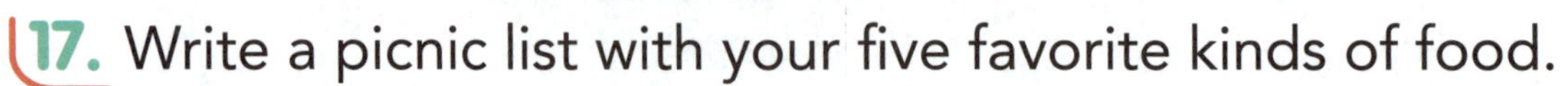

____

____

____

Say with Me!

Picnics are magic with fantastic breadsticks.

RESPECT NATURE, NO WASTING!

18. Look at the picture and talk to your classmates. 

Loch o' the Lowes
Picnic Site
Overnight vehicular camping is not permitted
Please take your litter home
Please respect the landscape

Loch of the Lowes Picnic Site, Yarrow Valley, Borders, Scotland, UK

Cornerstone Photos/Alamy/Fotoarena

19. In groups, create a logo in support of nature conservation.

20. Check the true sentences about the park.

a) ◯ The park is in Scotland.

b) ◯ Overnight vehicular camping is permitted.

c) ◯ Take your litter home.

d) ◯ Respect the landscape.

CHECK YOUR PROGRESS

AWESOME! ◯ 

GOOD JOB! ◯ 

I CAN DO BETTER. ◯ 

TIME TO LEARN ABOUT
OUTDOOR ACTIVITIES

1. Read and answer the questions.

BENEFITS OF CYCLING

Available at: https://www.ontarioparks.com/parksblog/five-outdoor-activities-improve-health/. Accessed on: Febr. 28, 2022.

a) Which outdoor activity do you prefer?

b) Are you happy when you practice this outdoor activity?

c) Do you prefer to practice this outdoor activity with your friends?

d) Where do you practice this outdoor activity?

2. Read the texts and number the pictures.  

1. I'm Jessica. I'm the girl in a red T-shirt. I love to play soccer with my friends at the park near my house. Grass and trees make me happy!
2. I'm Carlos. The 413 boy! I love to run. It is good for my body and for my mind! I can make new friends too!
3. I'm Pedro. I'm 12. My favorite outdoor activity is skateboarding. It boosts my mood and strengthens my body.
4. I'm Mayra and my favorite outdoor activity is listening to music. In this picture, I am relaxed and happy!

a

Kaspars Grinvalds/Shutterstock

b

Africa Studio/Shutterstock

c

Dean Drobot/Shutterstock

d

a katz/Shutterstock

MY FAVORITE OUTDOOR ACTIVITY IS...

3. Present some pictures of you practicing outdoor activities. 

UNIT

6 A BIRTHDAY PARTY

1. Listen and act out.  

Carol is organizing her birthday party.

Hello! Is that you, Kitty?
Yes! Hello, Carol!

Would you like to come to my birthday party, Kitty?

Sure! When is your birthday?

Marcos Mello/Arquivo da editora

It's next Sunday, April 25th.
What time is the party?
It starts at 4:00 p.m.
Where is the party?
At home – 24 Ford Street.
OK! Thanks, Carol!
You're welcome, Kitty.
See you on Sunday. Bye!
Bye-bye, Carol!

FINDING OUT

Birthday invitation

2. Read Amanda's birthday invitation and complete the chart. Then listen and check your answers.

YOU'RE INVITED TO MY
Birthday Party
22 AUGUST ★ 5 PM
Let's celebrate my 11th birthday!
You are my special guest!
Sunday - August 22nd.
From 5:00 p.m. to 10:00 p.m.
334 Captain Parker Road.
We will have hamburgers, pizza, ice cream and other delicious food.
Don't miss it!
RSVP at 201-2235.
yusufdemirci/Shutterstock

Name	Amanda
Age	
When	
Where	
What time	
Food	

3. Listen, stick and say.

Planning a birthday party

Things

balloons

birthday hat

candles

cake

sandwiches

sweets

Actions

dance

greet guests

open gifts

play games

sing Happy Birthday

talk with friends

4. Circle the words and write.

Banco de Imagens/Arquivo da editora

ACTIONS	THINGS

5. Listen, point and say.   

Ordinal numbers

1st first	2nd second	3rd third	4th fourth	5th fifth
6th sixth	7th seventh	8th eighth	9th ninth	10th tenth
11th eleventh	12th twelfth	13th thirteenth	14th fourteenth	15th fifteenth
16th sixteenth	17th seventeenth	18th eighteenth	19th nineteenth	20th twentieth
21st twenty-first	22nd twenty-second	23rd twenty-third	24th twenty-fourth	30th thirtieth
				31st thirty-first

6. Complete the sentences using ordinal numbers. 

a) A is the ______________ letter of the alphabet.

b) H is the ______________ letter of the alphabet.

c) The ______________ letter of the alphabet is B.

d) C is the ______________ letter of the alphabet.

e) The ______________ letter of the alphabet is F.

f) X is the ______________ letter of the alphabet.

LISTENING AND ORAL PRACTICE

7. Listen and number.

a)

Alex Andrei/Shutterstock

b)

Karl Allgaeuer/Shutterstock

c)

Nata-Lia/Shutterstock

d)

Timmary/Shutterstock

e)

Pirina/Shutterstock

f)

Pressmaster/Shutterstock

8. Listen and say the months.

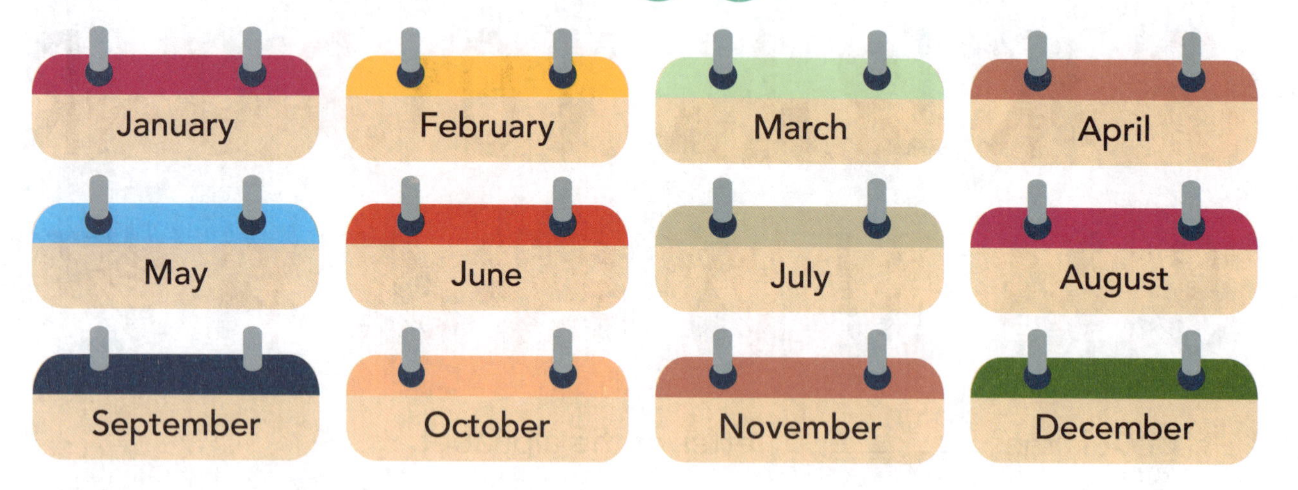

9. Listen and complete with their birthday months.

a) It's on ______________ 25th.

b) It's on ______________ 26th.

c) It's on ______________ 1st.

d) It's on ______________ 4th.

e) It's on ______________ 16th.

10. Complete, listen and act out.
a)
_______ your name?
My _______ is Miss Polly Jones.
b)
_______ old are you, Miss Jones?
I'm _______ years old.
c)
_______ is your birthday?
It's on _______ 16th.
_______ is your job?
I am a _______.
d)
_______ students are there in your classroom?
There are _______.
e)
And... _______ is it?
It's _______ o'clock.
It's time to start our class!
OK! Thanks for the interview, Miss Jones!
Ilustrações: Marcos Mello/Arquivo da editora
Eighty-nine 89

LANGUAGE ACTIVITIES

Writing dates

11. Write the dates using ordinal numbers. 

The first day of January/
January 1st (January the first)

The fourth day of February/
February 4th (February the fourth)

a) The first day of February: ____________________

b) The fifth day of April: ____________________

c) The tenth day of September: ____________________

d) The twentieth day of November: ____________________

e) The thirty-first day of December: ____________________

12. Choose the correct questions to the answers. 

What is your name? • What is this? • What day is today?
What time is it? • What color is your book? • What is your job?

a) ____________________
My name is Miss Polly Jones.

b) ____________________
My book is yellow.

c) ____________________
I'm a teacher.

d) ____________________
It's three o'clock.

e) ____________________
It's my book.

f) ____________________
Today is Monday.

13. Write the addresses.

There is a birthday party at Lucy's house. Melissa and Karen are checking the addresses.

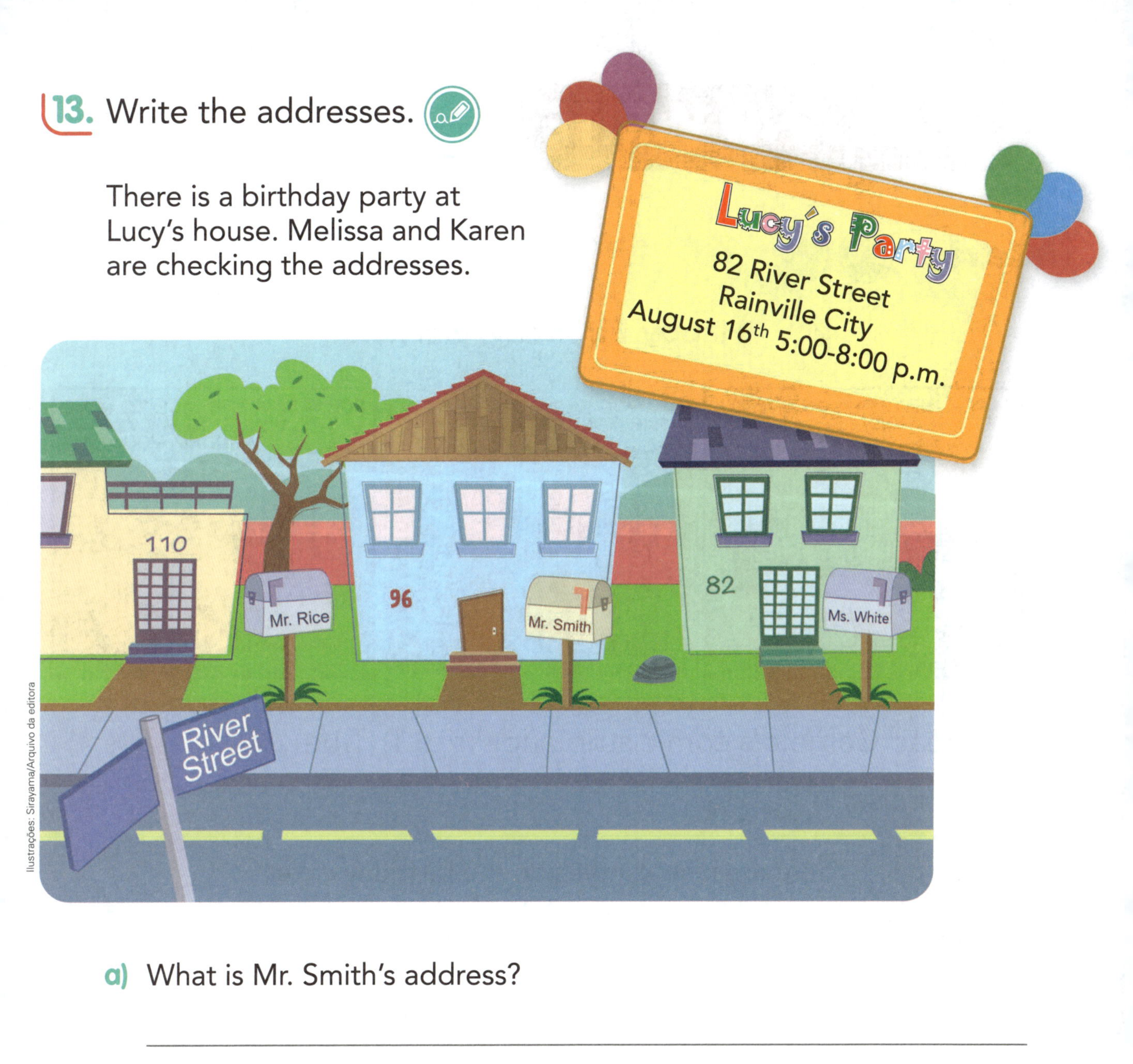

a) What is Mr. Smith's address?

____

b) What is Lucy White's address?
Lucy White's address is _______________________________.

Now it is your turn.

c) What is your address? My address is ____________________

____.

d) What is your best friend's address? My best friend's address is

____.

READ AND WRITE

Text 1  

Happy Birthday, Garfield!

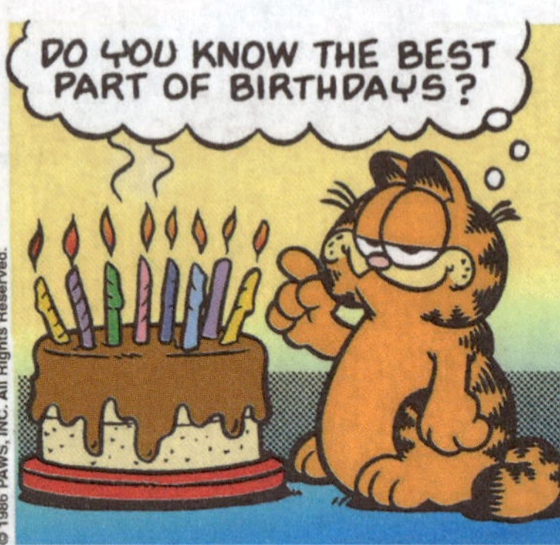

14. Read Garfield's comic strip and write **T** (True) or **F** (False).  

a) ◯ There are nine candles on the birthday cake.

b) ◯ There are four friends with Garfield.

c) ◯ Garfield is happy, the world is revolving around him today.

d) ◯ Garfield does not like birthday parties.

e) ◯ Garfield is eight years old.

15. Check the correct answer. 

a) Do you like birthday parties?
◯ Yes.
◯ No.

b) What do you prefer?
◯ Go to a friend's birthday party.
◯ Enjoy yourself in your own birthday party.

Text 2  

Chocolate Balls Recipe

Ingredients

- 1 package of milk biscuits
- 3 tablespoons of cocoa powder
- 1 box of condensed milk (395 g)
- 1 package of chocolate sprinkles for coating the balls

Method

1. Crush the biscuits.
2. Mix all ingredients together in a bowl.
3. Roll into small balls.
4. Roll each ball in chocolate sprinkles.
5. Put the balls in the refrigerator to cool.
6. Put them in a plate to serve.

Quick and easy
Great for kids' parties
Preparation time: 15 minutes

16. Number the recipe steps. Then circle the verbs.  

LightField Studios/Shutterstock

Africa Studio/Shutterstock

DeymosHR/Shutterstock

Ariadne Barroso/Shutterstock

hsunny/Shutterstock

( ) Roll the mixture into small balls.

( ) Crush the biscuits.

( ) Mix all ingredients together in a bowl.

( ) Put them in a plate to serve.

( ) Roll each ball in chocolate sprinkles.

Now you, write your favorite recipe and illustrate it.

LET'S SING!

For he's a jolly good fellow!

For he's a jolly good fellow, for he's a jolly good fellow
For he's a jolly good fellow (pause), which nobody can deny
Which nobody can deny, which nobody can deny
For he's a jolly good fellow, for he's a jolly good fellow
For he's a jolly good fellow (pause), which nobody can deny
(2×)

Studio Romantic/Shutterstock

17. Look at the picture and write **T** (True) or **F** (False).

a) ◯ There are twelve guests in this party.

b) ◯ There are two boys and three girls in the picture.

c) ◯ There are only three guests with birthday hats.

d) ◯ There is a decorated birthday cake on the table.

e) ◯ There are a lot of candles on the cake.

Say with Me!

Elizabeth's Birthday is on the third Thursday of this month.

18. Look at the picture and talk to your classmates. 

Rido/Shutterstock

19. Now, in groups, read, discuss and draw.   

How to be a good friend:

watch movies
play together
listen
be kind
share
take care
help each other
tell stories

CHECK YOUR PROGRESS

AWESOME! 

GOOD JOB! 

I CAN DO BETTER. 

REVIEW

1. Check the items you see in the picture.

What about a Picnic?

- Take the picnic basket and a tablecloth.
- Take some sandwiches, bananas, watermelon, apples and water.
- Go to the countryside or a park with your family or teacher and friends.
- Choose the shade of a big tree.
- Take out the tablecloth and sit down.
- Eat and drink.
- Enjoy yourselves!

Alex Mares-Manton/Getty Images

◯ plates	◯ picnic basket	◯ spoons
◯ fruits	◯ knives	◯ bottle of water
◯ soda	◯ forks	◯ plastic cups

2. Complete the sentences using the words from the box.

plastic cups • water • picnic • plates • sandwiches • shade

a) There are many __________ and __________ on the tablecloth.

b) It's better to choose the ________ of a big tree to have a ________ .

c) There are some fruits and __________ to eat and __________ to drink.

3. Look at Kitty's birthday invitation. Now you! Create your own invitation.

Graphicartist26/Shutterstock

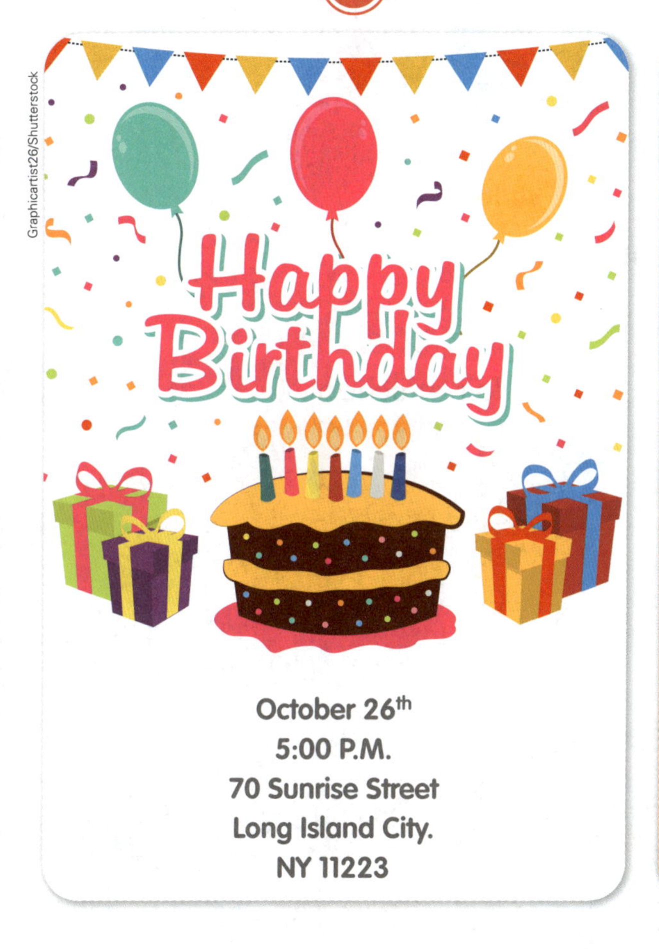

Happy Birthday
October 26th
5:00 P.M.
70 Sunrise Street
Long Island City.
NY 11223

4. Unscramble the sentences. 

a) birthday / is / this / a / cake.

____

b) guests / the / are / here.

____

c) balloons / are / the / colored.

____

d) your / when / birthday / is / ?

____

UNIT

7 A CULTURAL FAIR

1. Listen and act out.  

The teacher and the kids are organizing a cultural fair at school.

Hello! Good morning, class!
Good morning, teacher!

Today we will plan the cultural fair of this year.
Hurray!!!

Marcos Mello/Arquivo da editora

When is the fair, Ms. Jones?
It's on Saturday, November 9th.
NOVEMBER
9
Students, stay in small groups, please.
Can we choose the countries, Ms. Jones?
Sure! Each group chooses a different country and researches it.
Teacher, we can have food, dances, flags, a parade...
And we can decorate a panel about each country.
Yes, Jim!
OK!
We can display items related to the countries!
This cultural fair is a great time for students and community! Hands on!

Countries, nationalities and languages

Country	Brazil	Argentina	Italy	Mexico	Spain	Germany
Nationality	Brazilian	Argentinian	Italian	Mexican	Spanish	German
Language	Portuguese	Spanish	Italian	Spanish	Spanish	German

2. Look at the chart and complete. Then listen and check your answers.

a) I'm Pedro. I'm from Brazil.
I'm Brazilian. I speak Portuguese.

Pollyana Ventura/ Getty Images

b) I'm Paula. I'm from Argentina.

I'm ________________. I speak ________________.

Jupiter Candy/ Shutterstock

c) I'm Luigi. I'm from Italy.

I'm ________________. I speak ________________.

UMB-O/Shutterstock

d) I'm Juan. I'm from Mexico.

I'm ________________. I speak ________________.

Dannie Walls/Corbis/ Getty Images

e) I'm Talia. I'm from Spain.

I'm ________________. I speak ________________.

Oleksii Gavryliuk/ Shutterstock

f) I'm Frieda. I'm from Germany.

I'm ________________. I speak ________________.

Uschi Hering/ Shutterstock

3. Listen, stick and say.   

Countries and flags

Do you know these flags? Which countries are they? What do you know about these countries?

Australia

Brazil

Canada

China

England

India

Japan

New Zealand

Portugal

Russia

South Africa

The United States of America

4. Write the name of the country and the nationality. 

Julinzy/Shutterstock

____
____

Michael Roeder/Shutterstock

____
____

Maximumvector/Shutterstock

____
____

Loveshop/Shutterstock

____
____

Globe Turner/Shutterstock

____
____

Lukasz Stefanski/Shutterstock

____
____

5. Circle the names of the countries from activity 4. Then, complete the sentence.

Banco de Imagens/Arquivo da editora

Fonte: IBGE.

These countries are in ______________________, ______________________, ______________________ and ______________________.

LISTENING AND ORAL PRACTICE

6. Listen and number.

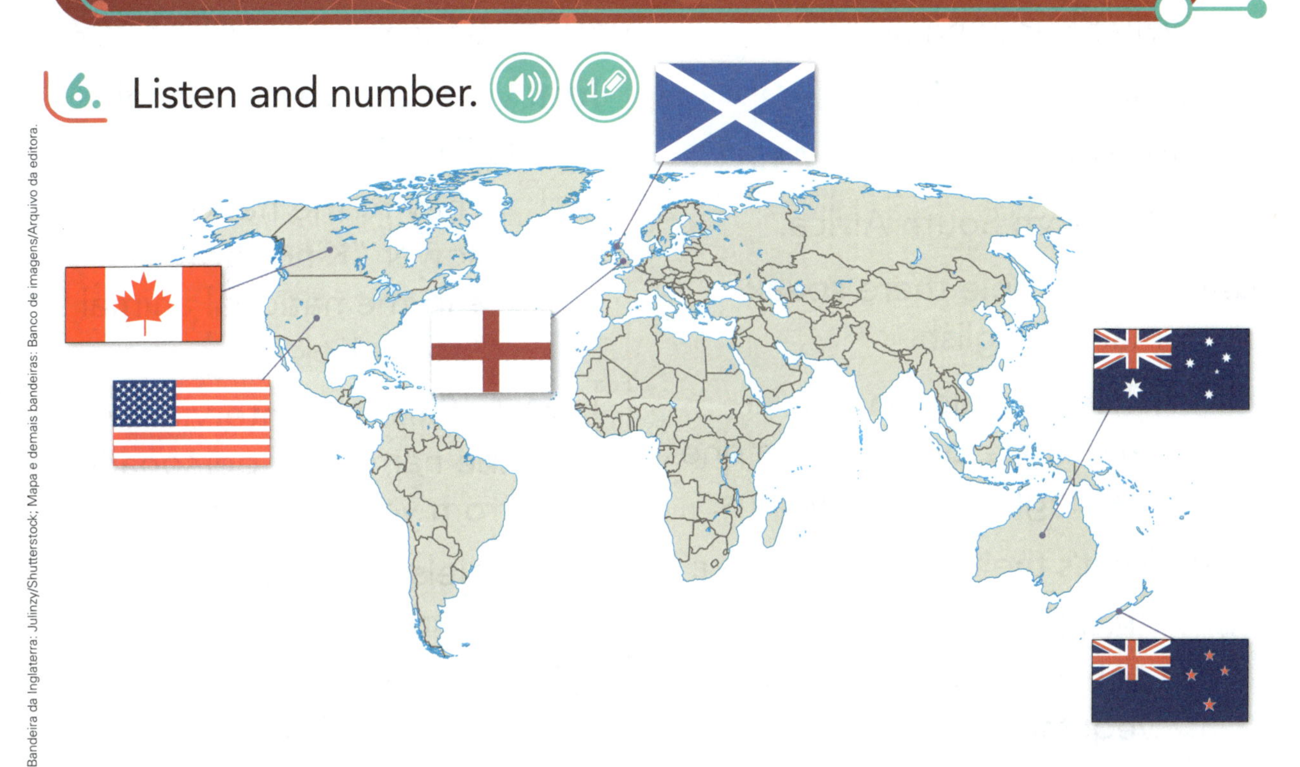

Bandeira da Inglaterra: Julinzy/Shutterstock; Mapa e demais bandeiras: Banco de imagens/Arquivo da editora.

A

Mostovyi Sergii Igorevich/Shutterstock

B

Milosz Maslanka/Shutterstock

C

imagevixen/Shutterstock

D

maziarz/Shutterstock

E

BorisVetshev/Shutterstock

F

Kiwi: didora/Shutterstock; pássaro: Aga Es/Shutterstock

7. Listen and act out.  

Leo: What's your name?

Akin: My name is Akin.

Leo: Where are you from, Akin?

Akin: I'm from South Africa.

Julie: And people there speak mainly English.

Akin: There are eleven official languages, but the main ones are English and Afrikaans.

Julie: What's the typical food there?

Akin: "Potjiekos", a traditional dish made with meat and vegetables.

Jim: What is the most popular sport?

Akin: Soccer.

Jim: What are their national symbols?

Akin: They're the national flower "King Protea" and the national animal "springbok".

Leo: To finish the interview, say the name of a personality from your country.

Akin: Nelson Mandela and Wangari Maathai.

Julie: Oh! Akin, thank you for the interview.

Akin: You're welcome!

8. Now, complete the chart about South Africa.

SOUTH AFRICA

Population: ___*over 60 million*___

Languages: ______________________________

____

Food: ______________ Sport: ______________

Symbols: the national flower "______________"/

the national animal "______________"

Personality: ______________________________

Interrogative pronouns

9. In pairs, ask these questions to your classmate.

Where are you from?	______________________
What is your nationality?	______________________
What is your favorite sport?	______________________
What language(s) do you speak?	______________________
What is the national symbol of your country?	______________________

10. Write questions about Giovanna.

BestPhotoStudio/Shutterstock

Viacheslav Lopatin/Shutterstock

joyfull/Shutterstock

a) ______________________? I'm from Italy.

b) ______________________? I'm Italian.

c) ______________________? I speak Italian.

d) ______________________? They are green, white and red.

Prepositions of place

in • on • next to • under • behind • between

11. Match. Where is the matrioska?

12. Read and circle the correct preposition. 

a) The Brazilian "berimbau" is on/in the table.

b) The Japanese "kimono" is in/on the box.

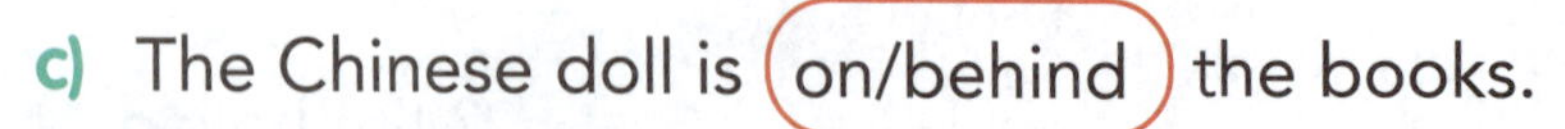
c) The Chinese doll is on/behind the books.

d) The Argentinian flag is under/behind the window.

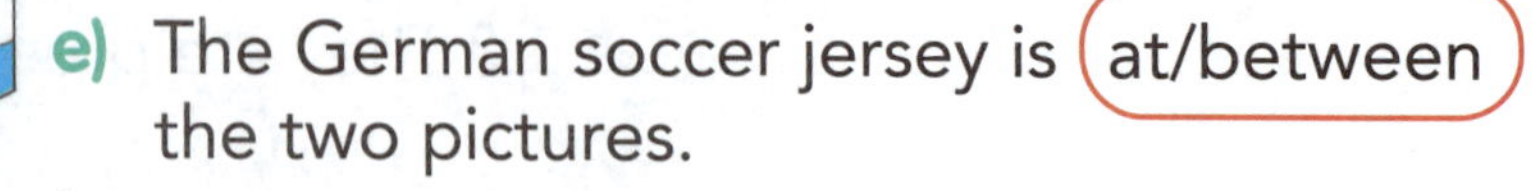
e) The German soccer jersey is at/between the two pictures.

Ilustrações: Ilustra Cartoon/Arquivo da editora

READ AND WRITE

Text  

Yohanna

AleCasa77/Shutterstock

Seven-year-old Yohanna lives in Addis Ababa, the capital of Ethiopia. It is the fourth-largest city in Africa. Yohanna's two favorite place to visit are Edna shopping mall and the Lion Zoo.

Family

Yohanna lives with her mother, a teacher, her father, an aircraft technician, and her two younger siblings. Yohanna's family is Christian.

Favorite food

Yohanna's family often eats **wat**, which is an Ethiopian stew. They serve it with roasted lamb, rice and a flatbread called **injera**.

Playtime

When she's not at school, Yohanna likes to play jump-roping games with her friends. She also enjoys playing soccer with her brother Abemelek.

Children Just Like Me: A New Celebration of Children Around the World. Written by Catherine Saunders, Sam Priddy, and Katy Lennon. Published in the United States by DK Publishing, New York: 2016.

13. Check the correct answers. 

a) ◯ Yohanna is seven years old and comes from Addis Ababa, the capital of Ethiopia.

b) ◯ She speaks English and French.

c) ◯ Yohanna likes to play jump-roping and soccer.

d) ◯ Her favorite food is wat.

e) ◯ Her family is big. There are seven members in her family.

14. Write to a friend about yourself. 

LET'S SING!

15. Listen and circle the correct word.

Where are you from?

It doesn't (better – matter) where you are from
Brazil, Peru, Argentina,
U.S.A., Canada, China.

It doesn't matter (where – there) you are from
U.K., Mexico, Poland,
Italy, Russia, Holland.

It doesn't matter where you are (from – come)
South Africa, Japan, Australia,
New Zealand, Italy, India.

We are always making new (sends – friends)
We all live in the same (world – word)
We are all (better – together)
'Cause the world is only (one – some)!

melitas/Shutterstock

173 WB

Say with Me!

We are all born in a different way,
how we look and what we say,
what we like and the things we do,
No matter!
The world is colorful all the way!

YES TO CULTURAL DIVERSITY!

16. Look at the picture and talk to a classmate. 

wavebreakmedia/Shutterstock

17. Read and number the pictures. In groups, create a poster about cultural diversity.  

Culture is...

1. clothes and dressing
2. food
3. language
4. religion
5. folk art
6. celebrations
7. jokes
8. manners
9. child-rearing methods
10. medical cure
11. working schedule

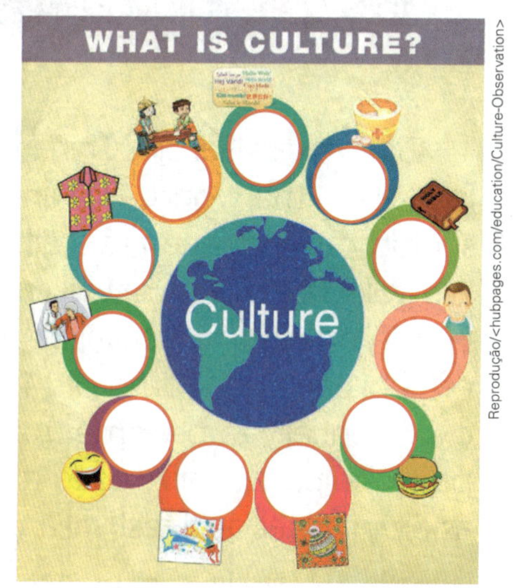

Reprodução/<hubpages.com/education/Culture-Observation>

CHECK YOUR PROGRESS

AWESOME! 

GOOD JOB! 

I CAN DO BETTER. 

TIME TO LEARN ABOUT

FESTIVALS OF THE WORLD

WHAT IS YOUR FAVORITE FESTIVAL?

1. Read and match to the pictures.

1

Kristin F. Ruhs/Shutterstock

2

Giusparta/Shutterstock

( ) Every year Harbin, China is home to one of the most fascinating ice festivals in the world. The annual winter festival features massive ice and snow sculptures and features a different theme each year. At night the ice sculptures are colourfully illuminated and appear to come to life as a breathtaking ice city. Typically, the festival begins on January 5 and usually runs until the end of February, beginning of March weather permitting. Over time it has grown exponentially to become the largest ice and snow festival in the world. In the past, the participants used to be predominantly Chinese, but since its induction as an international festival and competition things have changed.

Available at: https://www.thepinnaclelist.com/articles/harbin-international-snow-ice-festival-illuminated-awe-inspiring-winter-wonderland-china/. Accessed on Mar. 4, 2022.

( ) Holi is a popular ancient Hindu festival, also known as the "Festival of Love", the "Festival of Colours", and the "Festival of Spring". Holi celebrates the arrival of spring, the end of winter, the blossoming of love and for many, it is a festive day to meet others, play and laugh, forget and forgive, and repair broken relationships. The festival also celebrates the beginning of a good spring harvest season. It lasts for a night and a day.

Available at: https://kids.kiddle.co/Holi. Accessed on Mar. 4, 2022.

MY FAVORITE FESTIVAL IS...

2. In groups, choose your favorite festival and present it to your classmates.

Chinese New Year, China.

Maracatu Festivity and Tradition, Brazil.

Albuquerque International Balloon Fiesta, United States.

June Festivities, Brazil.

Maracatu Festivity and Tradition

The Maracatu is a carnival tradition created by the black population of Pernambuco, Brazil. The typical music consists in "gonguê" beat and "zabumba" rhythm, accompanied by the "cuíca," the "ganzá". Maracatu has its roots in the sugar fazendas and slave estates in 1674. Each year the crowning of the slave King and Queen was celebrated with music and dance and the involvement of many of the "maracatu" participants in their own Afro-Brazilian cultures. This is one of the most colorful carnival festivals in Brazil.

Based on: https://artsandculture.google.com/story/maracatu-and-the-alagoas-warrior-afro-brazilian-festivities-museu-afro-brasil/BwWBFGxbua7nIQ?hl=en and https://www.solsamba.co.uk/brazilian-music/maracatu/.

UNIT 8

YOU CAN HELP THE PLANET

1. Listen and act out.  

Marcos Mello/Arquivo da editora

Oh, Tobby, turn off the tap to save water!
Oh, yes, dad!
What are you doing, Leo?
I'm organizing paper and plastic garbage for recycling.
Yeah! You are helping the planet!
Great! You're very "green".

FINDING OUT

2. Listen and number. Then circle three options that you can include in your daily routine.

Go Green!

What does it mean to "Go Green"? To "Go Green" means to make Earth conscious decisions when buying and using products or doing things to help the Earth. There are many fun and simple things you can do everyday to help the planet.
Try some of these ideas! [...]

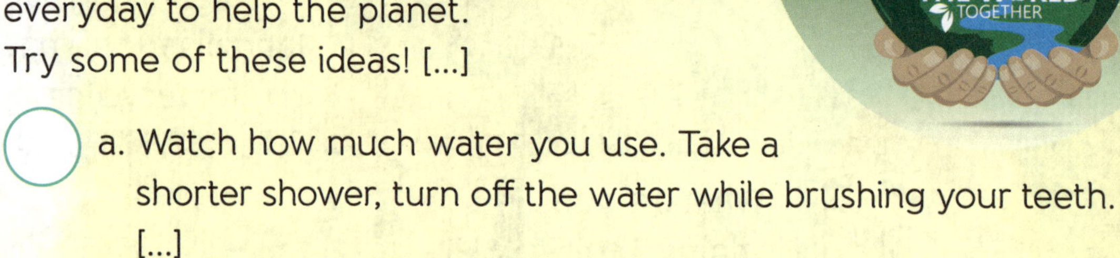

kowition/Shutterstock

( ) a. Watch how much water you use. Take a shorter shower, turn off the water while brushing your teeth. [...]

( ) b. Turn off the lights when you leave the room. [...]

( ) c. Unplug electronic items when they are not in use. [...]. Unplugging things such as radios, TV and video games will save energy and money.

( ) d. Bring your own cloth bags when shopping. Did you know that it takes 14 million trees to make all the paper bags used in the US each year? [...]

( ) e. Always use refillable bottles instead of plastic water bottles. Did you know that only 12% of plastic bottles are recycled? The other 88% end up in landfills.

( ) f. Recycle your garbage! [...] Separate recyclable items from your other garbage. Find out from your town when recycle garbage is picked up or bring your items to a drop off location.

Extracted from: www.kidsplayandcreate.com/fun-go-green-ideas-for-kids-fun-ways-to-help-the-earth-for-kids-earth-day-activities-for-kids/. Accessed on: March 5, 2022.

Ilustra Cartoon/Arquivo da editora

3. Listen, stick and say.

What are you doing?

sleeping

turning on/off

drawing

waking up

washing the hands

switching on/off

cleaning

watching TV

reading

walking

working

writing

running

talking

resting

playing video game

eating

drinking

4. Look at the picture and number.

( ) Clara is cleaning the garage.

( ) Tom is switching off the tap.

( ) Paul is washing his hands.

( ) Mr. Wells is resting.

( ) Tina is eating.

( ) Matt is waking up.

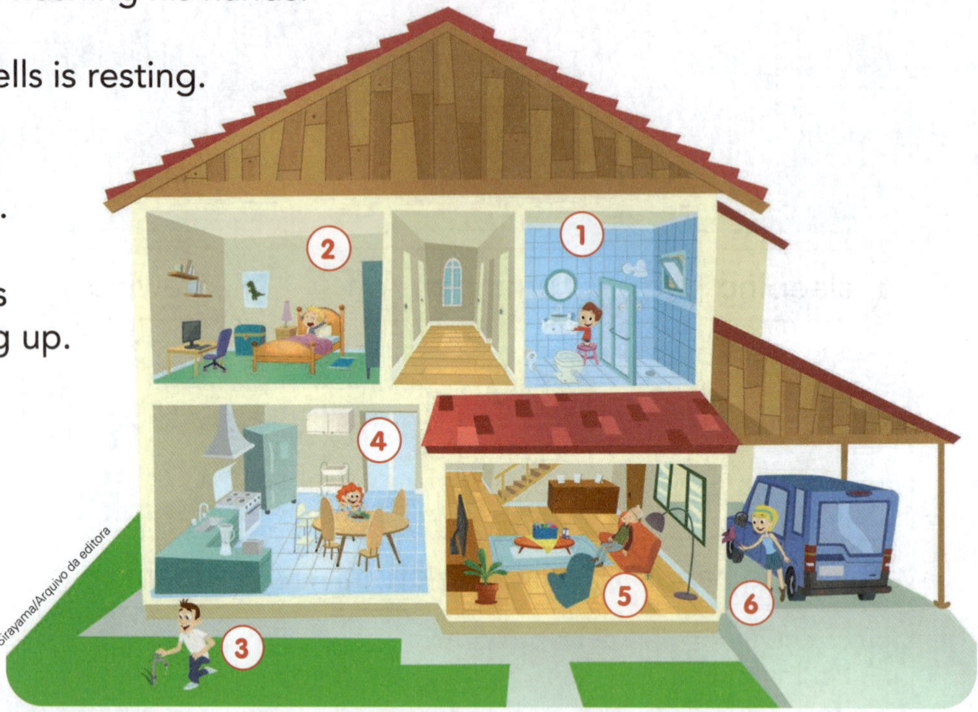

Sirayama/Arquivo da editora

5. In pairs, write ten actions using these letters.

A C D E G I K L
N O P R S T V W

_______________ _______________

_______________ _______________

_______________ _______________

_______________ _______________

_______________ _______________

6. Complete the sentences gaps according to the pictures. 

writing • drinking • reading • washing • drawing • eating • sleeping

Robert Kneschke/Shutterstock

He is __________ water.

Marcel Jancovic/Shutterstock

The girl is __________ her hands.

Ramona Heim/Shutterstock

The baby is __________.

AS photostudio/Shutterstock

The woman is __________ the newspaper.

Bricolage/Shutterstock

The boy is __________ a cookie.

T-Design/Shutterstock

Susan is __________ a house, a car etc.

stockfour/Shutterstock

The teacher is __________ on the board.

LISTENING AND ORAL PRACTICE

7. Listen and make an **X**.  

a)

Dmytro Zinkevych/Shutterstock

( ) yes ( ) no

b)

mimagephotography/Shutterstock

( ) yes ( ) no

c)

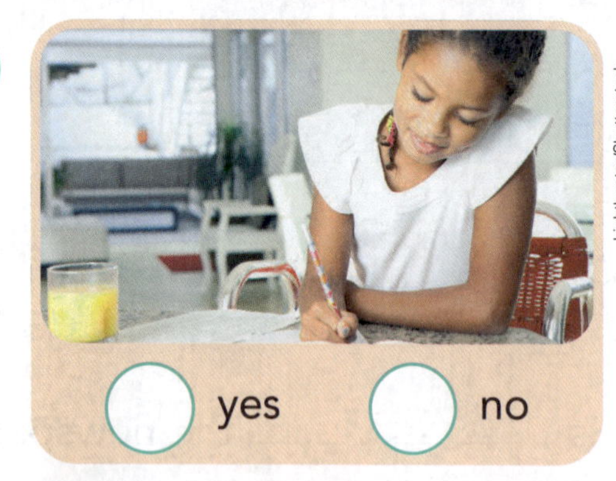

Lighthunter/Shutterstock

( ) yes ( ) no

d)

hanapon1002/Shutterstock

( ) yes ( ) no

e)

Lighthunter/Shutterstock

( ) yes ( ) no

f)

Dmitry Kalinovsky/Shutterstock

( ) yes ( ) no

g)

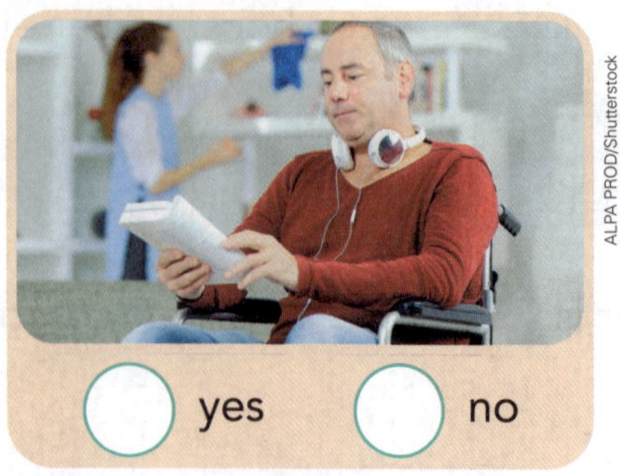

ALPA PROD/Shutterstock

( ) yes ( ) no

h)

PeopleImages.com - Yuri A/Shutterstock

( ) yes ( ) no

8. Listen, complete and act out.

Mark: Hello!

George: ______________! How are ______________, Mark?

Mark: ______________ fine, George, and you?

George: I'm fine, thanks. What ______________ you doing?

Mark: I'm hungry. I'm ______________ a sandwich. And you, what are you ______________?

George: I am ______________ video game. Come home and play with me!

Mark: Oh, ______________..., I have a lot of things to do now. Maybe later.

George: OK! I'm ______________ for you. Bye!

Mark: Bye, George! ______________ for inviting me to ______________ with you.

LukaM/Shutterstock

Zurijeta/Shutterstock

9. Listen and complete the sentences with the words from the box.

important • products • new things • recycling • papers • plastic • materials • bin box • newspapers • magazines

a) Kids, do you have a special ______________ in your classroom where you place used ______________? [...]

b) What is ______________?

c) Recycling is taking used ______________ like cans, plastic, ______________, ______________, glass bottles and turning them into new ______________ we can use again.

d) So, why is recycling ______________?

e) Well... instead of making an entirely new item each time we need something like ______________ jugs, bottles and cardboards and make ______________ [...]

LANGUAGE ACTIVITIES

The Present Continuous

To be + verb + **ing**

What are you doing?
I am reading a book.

Sirayama/Arquivo da editora

10. Look at the pictures and answer the questions. 

work • eat • rest • talk • wake up

A

AS photostudio/Shutterstock

What is she doing?

She is working.

B

carballo/Shutterstock

What is he doing?

___

C

fizkes/Shutterstock

What are they doing?

___

YAKOBCHUK VIACHESLAV/Shutterstock

What are they doing?

____

NDAB Creativity/Shutterstock

What is she doing?

____

11. Read and match the sentence halves.  

Cultura Motion/Shutterstock

Let's help the planet!

- Use towels, rags and sponges to clean the house.
- Use cloth grocery bags for shopping. They save energy and resources.
- Use plastic food containers to take lunch to school. They are more durable than plastic bags.
- Use rechargeable batteries in players, digital cameras and flashlights.

a) For shopping...

b) Plastic food containers are...

c) For players and digital cameras...

d) To clean the house...

( ) use towels, rags and sponges.

( ) more durable than plastic bags.

( ) use rechargeable batteries.

( ) use cloth grocery bags.

Text 1   

Take the quiz: How green are you?

[...] Work your way through these quick 10 questions and see just how green you really are. The answers are at the bottom – so enjoy finding out!

1. Do you switch off your TV/computer/ sound system at the wall?

a) Always.
b) Mostly.
c) Sometimes.

2. When you clean your teeth, do you let the water run?

a) Yes.
b) No!
c) Sometimes.

3. Do you grow your own food at home?

a) Yes – loads.
b) Yes, some.
c) No, not really.

4. How many of your home's light bulbs are low energy ones?

a) None / one or two.
b) About half.
c) All of them.

5. How much of your household waste do you recycle?

a) We put our bottles in the bottle bank.
b) As much as we can.
c) Most of what we can.

6. How did you travel to your last holiday?

a) By boat or train.
b) On foot or by bicycle.
c) By air.

7. How do you get to school?

a) Walk or cycle.
b) School bus.
c) Car.

8. Shower or bath?

a) Bath.
b) Shower.
c) Don't care.

9. Do you have a wildlife friendly garden?

a) We've got a bit of a wildlife corner, but it's nothing special.
b) I think we've got a bird box.
c) We've got bird boxes, a wildlife area, a pond and loads of plants for bees and butterflies.

10. How many times do you re-use the plastic bags shops people give you?

a) Once, maybe.
b) Several times.
c) Never take them; I always use my own bag.

[...]

Extracted from: https://ecofriendlykids.co.uk/how-green-are-you/. Accessed on: April 3rd, 2022.

How Did You Do?

22 to 30 – Deep Green! 16 to 21 – Emerald Green! 10 to 15 – Light Green!

Whatever shade of green you are, have fun being eco-friendly!

Text 2

Recycling & Facts

Recycling is when we take materials that we were going to throw away and put them through a process so they can be reused again.

Many things can be recycled such as paper, metal, plastic, glass and electrical equipment.

Recycling saves energy, is good for the environment, saves natural resources and saves space in landfills.

Recycling also saves money. It costs around $30 per ton to recycle. It costs $50 per ton to deliver garbage to a landfill and another $60-75 to incinerate (burn) it. [...]

Did you know that 75% of garbage is recyclable but we only recycle around 30%? [...]

Extracted from: www.kidsplayandcreate.com/teach-kids-abou-recycling-recycling-facts-for-kids. Accessed on: March 5, 2022.

12. Look at the pictures and number the steps of collecting garbage.

Ilustrações: Ilustra Cartoon/Arquivo da editora

2. selective collecting garbage • 4. manual sorting • 6. transport of the recycled material to industries • 3. transport by the garbage truck • 1. collecting garbage • 5. waste recycling and preparation of the recycled material

LET'S SING!

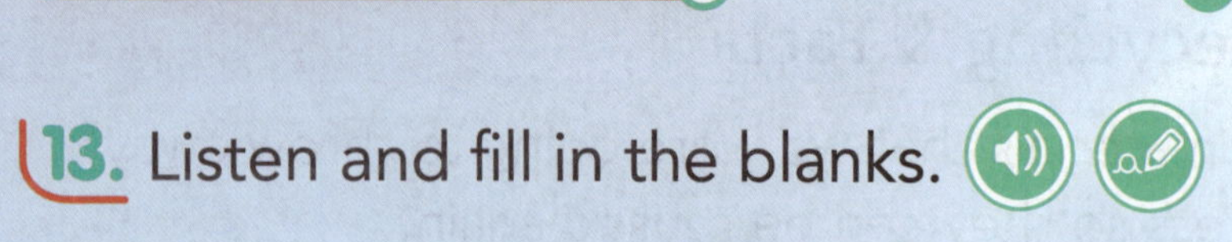

13. Listen and fill in the blanks.

WHAT A WONDERFUL WORLD

I see trees of ____________, red roses too

I see them bloom for me and ____________

And I think to myself what a wonderful ____________.

I see skies of ____________ and clouds of ____________

The bright blessed ____________, the dark sacred night

And I think to myself what a ____________ world.

The ____________ of the rainbow so pretty in the ____________

Are also on the faces of people going by

I see ____________ shaking hands sayin' "How do you do?"

They're really sayin' "I ____________ you".

175 WB

____________ hear babies cryin', ____________ watch them grow

They'll learn much more than I'll ever ____________

And I ____________ to myself ____________ a wonderful world.

Yes, I ____________ to myself what a wonderful ____________.

What a wonderful world. Bob Thiele, George David Weiss e George Douglas.

JBOY/Shutterstock

Say with Me!

I wonder if we can build a peaceful and wonderful world. I wonder!

PROTECT THE ENVIRONMENT!

14. Look at the picture and talk to your classmates.

24Novembers/Shutterstock

15. Read the text, underline the actions and circle their consequences.

If you turn off the lights,
You save energy.
If you switch off the tap,
You save water.

If you see a piece of litter,
Pick it up.
(And) you will make the planet
better.

16. In groups, create a slogan for a poster campaign on environment protection. Share it with your classmates.  

CHECK YOUR PROGRESS

AWESOME! 

GOOD JOB!

I CAN DO BETTER. 

REVIEW

1. Make an **X** to complete the sentences. 

a) They speak ◯ Portugal. ◯ Portuguese.

b) I am from ◯ Russia. ◯ Russian.

c) Where ◯ is ◯ are she from?

d) What's ◯ his ◯ your nationality? I am Chinese.

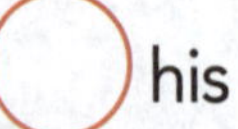

e) We are Brazilians. We speak ◯ Brazilian. ◯ Portuguese.

2. Complete the sentences with **in**, **on**, **under**, **between** or **behind**.

a) The Scottish flag is between the Brazilian and the Portuguese flags.

b) The English flag is ________ the table.

c) The Russian flag is ________ the boy.

d) The Spanish flag is ________ the window.

Ilustrações: Ilustra Cartoon/Arquivo da editora

3. Read the text and write **T** (True) or **F** (False).  

Today is Saturday

Kitty is studying and Tobby is playing with his toys.
Leo is playing soccer with Allan and Jim.
Mom and Dad are cleaning the kitchen.
Fido is sleeping in the dog house.
Grandpa and grandma are in the garden.
And the TV is turned on... Oh, gosh!

a) ◯ Carol and Tobby are studying.

b) ◯ Kitty and Jim are playing tennis.

c) ◯ Mom and dad are cleaning the kitchen.

d) ◯ Fido is sleeping in the dog house.

e) ◯ Grandpa and grandma are reading books.

f) ◯ The TV is turned off.

And you, what are you doing?

____

4. Unscramble the sentences. 

a) Kitty – is – tap – turning – off – the -.

____

b) they – recycling – the – are – garbage -.

____

c) lights – Leo – turning – is – on – the -.

____

EXTRA PRACTICE 1

1. Write the words in the correct column. 

Ilustra Cartoon/Arquivo da editora

School subjects	School objects	Colors	Numbers

2. Unscramble and match.  

a) aeeftriac ______________________________

b) ybralir ______________________________

c) umautodiri ______________________________

d) ymg ______________________________

e) ceSncie abl ______________________________

mattomedia KG/Shutterstock

Monkey Business Images/Shutterstock

Feel good studio/Shutterstock

Gorodenkoff/Shutterstock

Monkey Business Images/Shutterstock

3. Circle the odd words. 

a) English • Science • Geography • school • Math

b) Art • pencil • book • pen • eraser

c) twenty • fifty • forty • seventy • tree

d) Today • Sunday • Tuesday • Saturday • Monday

e) library • eraser • classroom • Art room • Robotics

EXTRA PRACTICE 2

1. Unscramble and match the words to the pictures.  

a) egt pu ______________________

b) ktae a oshrwe ______________________

c) bhrus hte tthee ______________________

d) ombc het irah ______________________

e) avhe rkbtfeaas ______________________

f) og ot hosolc ______________________

netbritish/Shutterstock

____

Ixepop/Shutterstock

____

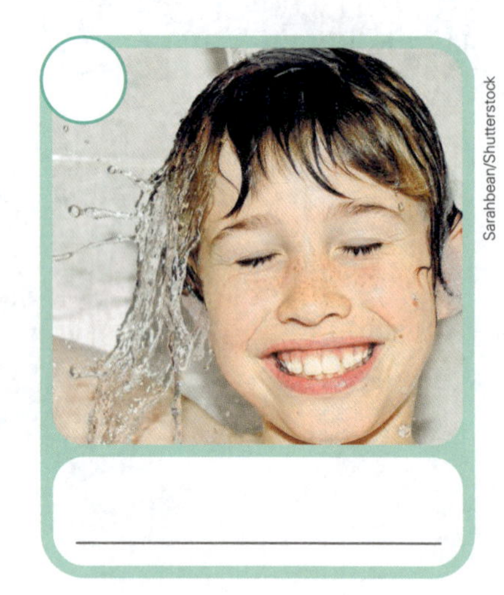
Sarahbean/Shutterstock

____

Casper1774 Studio/Shutterstock

____

TinnaPong/Shutterstock

____

Partha Pal/Stockbyte/Getty Images

____

2. Circle the odd expressions. Then write sentences using them.

a)

have breakfast • do my homework
have dinner • have lunch

Monkey Business Images/Shutterstock

I do my homework at 2:00 p.m.

b)

take a shower • watch TV
comb the hair • brush the teeth

Dani Liao Calvet/Shutterstock

c)

get up • midday • five o'clock
midnight • three thirty p.m.

Halfpoint/Shutterstock

d)

stand up • sit down • come here
silence, please • good morning

Halfpoint/Shutterstock

EXTRA PRACTICE 3

1. Write the sentences under the correct pictures. 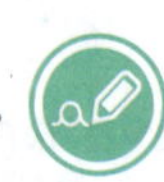

I'm tired. I can't do my homework.
My garden! What's this? I'm angry now!
It's my birthday. I'm happy!
I'm sad. I can't swim.

TY Lim/Shutterstock

wavebreakmedia/Shutterstock

SNAB/Shutterstock

Natalia Fedchenko/Shutterstock

2. Be creative! Write a mysterious message with emojis. 

Yefym Turkin/ Shutterstock

3. Interview four classmates: What are your favorite free time activities?

NAME:				

Ilustrações: Ilustra Cartoon/Arquivo da editora; skate: Reprodução/Acervo da editora.

4. Now write about your classmates. 

EXTRA PRACTICE 4

1. Break the code. Write a sentence for each picture. 

grandma and grandpa	watch	TV	grown-ups	a	Internet	of	talk	teenagers

and	children	chat	lot	bills	on	pay	work	the	to	friends

A

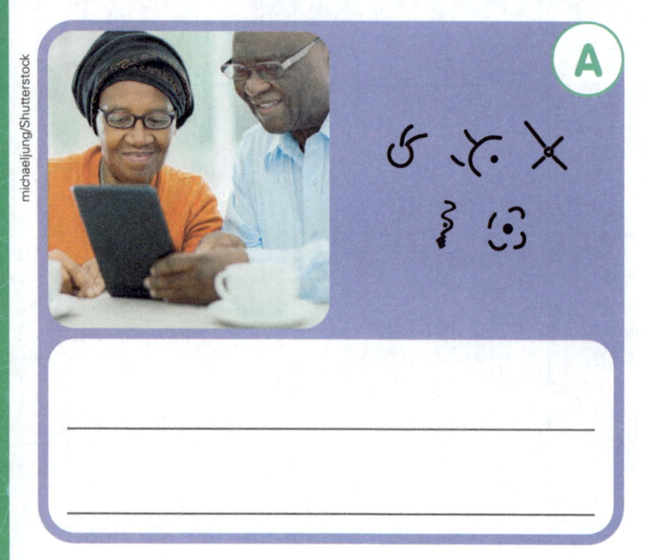

michaeljung/Shutterstock

B

Pitipat Usanakornkul/Shutterstock

C

Maryna Pleshkun/Shutterstock

D

Iakov Filimonov/Shutterstock

2. Complete the text by making an **X**.

a It's
- ◯ Monday.
- ◯ Tuesday.
- ◯ Wednesday.
- ◯ Thursday.
- ◯ Friday.
- ◯ Saturday.

b It's
- ◯ morning.
- ◯ afternoon.

c I am a
- ◯ teacher.
- ◯ student.

d I am at
- ◯ school.
- ◯ home.

e My English teacher is
- ◯ a man.
- ◯ a woman.

f I am doing
- ◯ English exercises.
- ◯ Science exercises.

3. Now copy the text in full and illustrate it.

____

____

____

____

EXTRA PRACTICE 5

1. Allan, Carol and Julie are at the snack bar. Look for the prices and complete their orders. Then answer the questions.

MENU
Tuna sandwich---$ 3
Hamburger--$ 4
Hot dog-----$ 4
Carrot cake-------$ 2
Potato chips---------$ 1
Fruit salad---------$ 1
Soda------------$ 2
Orange juice-----------$ 2
Lemonade-----$ 2

Ilustra Cartoon/Arquivo da editora

Allan:

a hamburger $ ___

a soda $ ___

a carrot cake $ ___

total $ ___

Carol:

a tuna sandwich $ ___

an orange juice $ ___

a fruit salad bowl $ ___

total $ ___

Julie:

a hot dog $ ___

potato chips $ ___

a lemonade $ ___

total $ ___

Ilustrações: Clau Souza/Arquivo da editora

a) Who spent more money? ◯ Allan ◯ Carol ◯ Julie

b) Who prefers healthy food? ◯ Allan ◯ Carol ◯ Julie

2. Fill in the blanks.

A

Artens/Shutterstock

There are a lot of ______________ in the ______________ .

B

ESB Professional/Shutterstock

The sun is ______________ in the ______________ .

C

winyuu/Shutterstock

______________ is the season of tree ______________ falling.

D

Pressmaster/Shutterstock

It's ______________ in the ______________ .

3. Look at the box of cookies and make an **X**.

alexat25/Shutterstock

a) The box of cookies is:

- ( ) green and black.
- ( ) red and black.
- ( ) white and blue.

b) The cookies are made of: ( ) chocolate. ( ) pure butter.

c) The shape of the cookies is: ( ) round. ( ) square.

d) These cookies are from: ( ) England. ( ) Scotland.

EXTRA PRACTICE 6

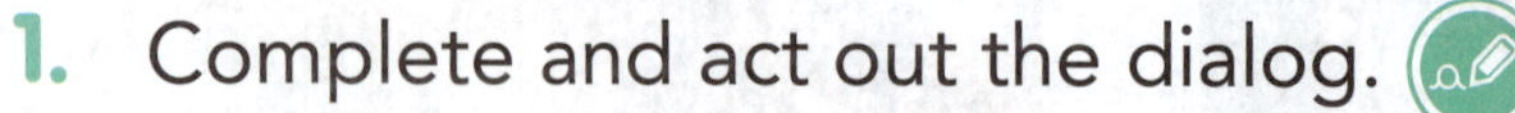

1. Complete and act out the dialog.  

bye-bye • welcome • when • Saturday • my house • time

Peter: ________ is your birthday party?

Claire: It's next Saturday.

Peter: At what ________ ?

Claire: Starts at 6:30 p.m.

Peter: Where is the party?

Claire: At ________ .

Peter: Thanks for inviting me!

Claire: You're ________ !

FatCamera/iStockphoto/Getty Images

Peter: See you on ________ .

Claire: I hope you can come!

Peter: For sure! Good-bye.

Claire: ________ !

2. Answer the questions. 

a) When is your birthday? ________

b) How old are you? ________

c) What's your address? ________

3. Complete the crossword. 

August • February • November • April •
March • July • June • September •
May • January • December • October

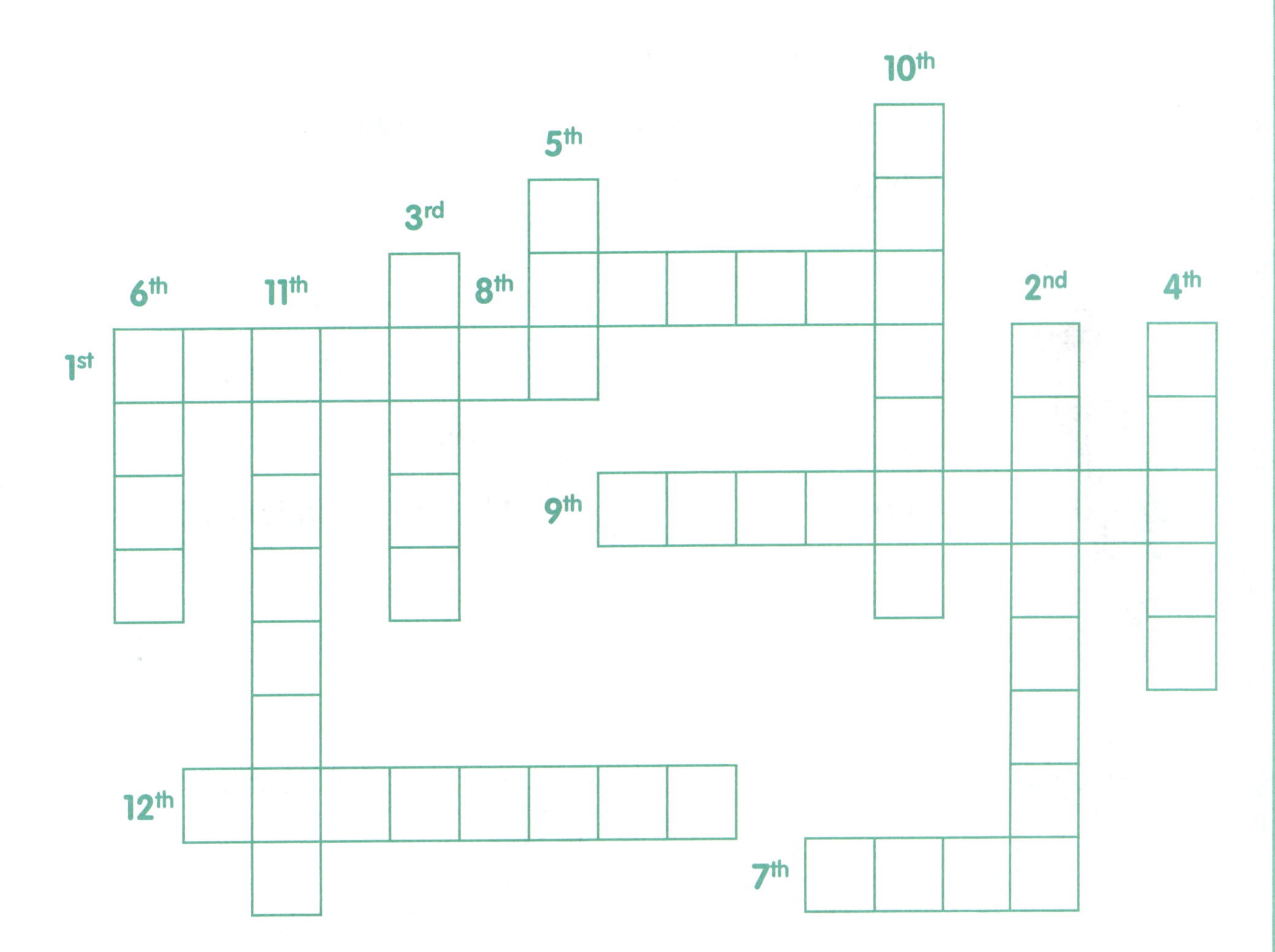

4. Complete the sentences. 

a) My birthday is in the 7th month of the year. It is in ______________.

b) December is the ______________________ month of the year.

c) The fifth day of April: _________________________.

d) Mother's Day is in ____________.

e) Independence Day in Brazil is on the seventh day of ____________.

EXTRA PRACTICE 7

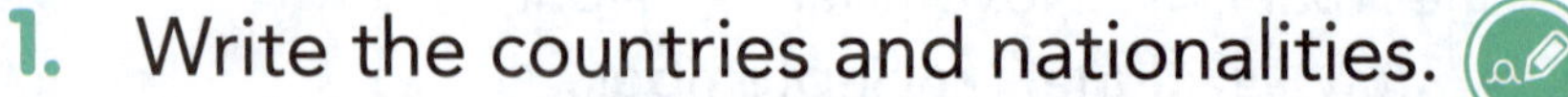

1. Write the countries and nationalities. 

1. Portugal	**4.** Italy
2. Canada	**5.** The United States of America
3. Argentina	**6.** Japan

1

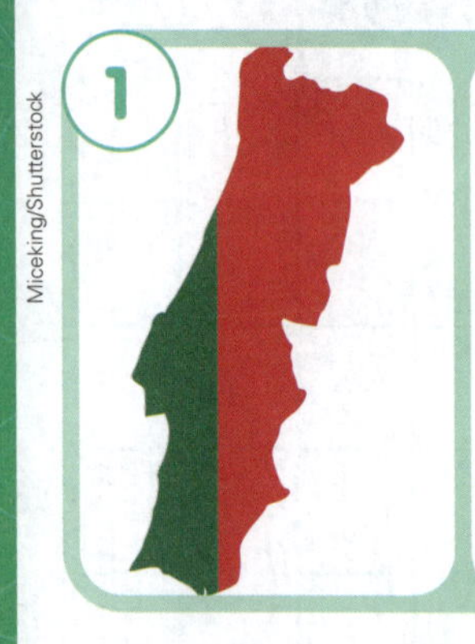

Miceking/Shutterstock

Country: ____________________

Nationality: ____________________

2

Miceking/Shutterstock

Country: ____________________

Nationality: ____________________

3

Miceking/Shutterstock

Country: ____________________

Nationality: ____________________

4

Miceking/Shutterstock

Country: ____________________

Nationality: ____________________

5

Miceking/Shutterstock

Country: ____________________

Nationality: ____________________

6

Miceking/Shutterstock

Country: ____________________

Nationality: ____________________

2. Write the countries's name. Then find and circle the nationalities.

Bandeira da Inglaterra: Julinzy/Shutterstock; demais bandeiras: Banco de imagens/Arquivo da editora

1

____

2

____

3

____

4

____

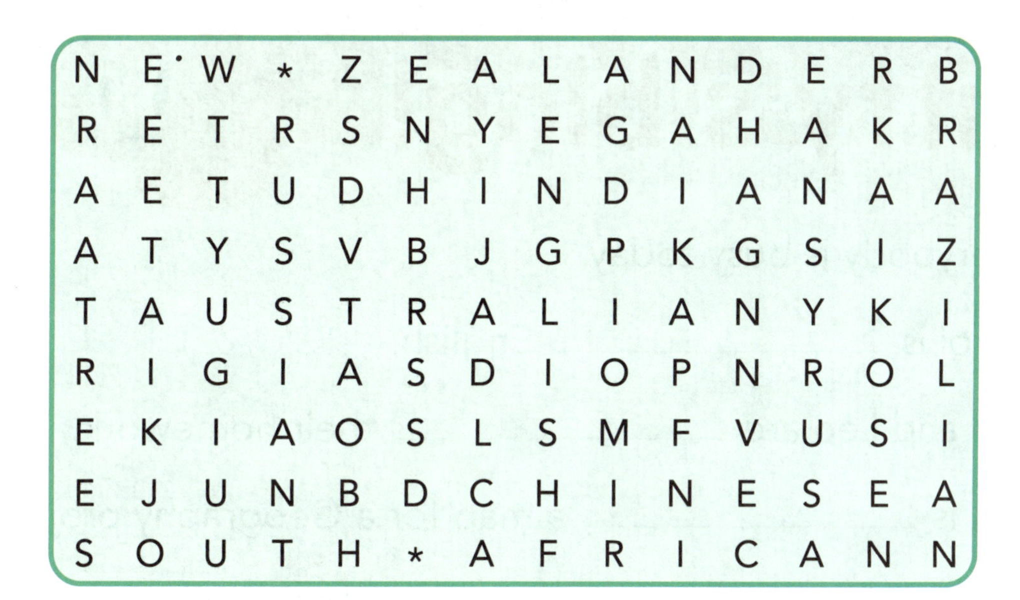

5

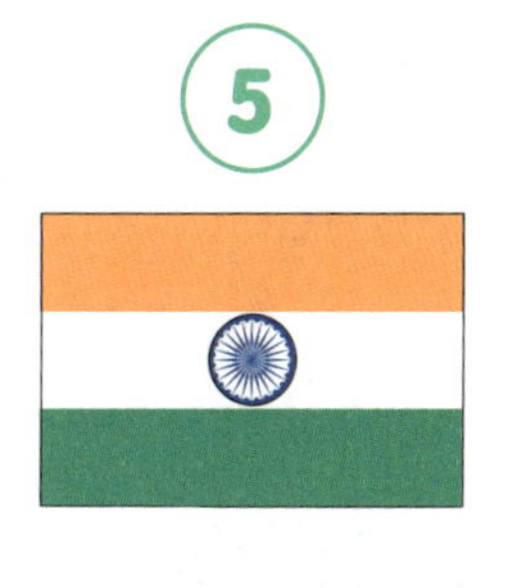

____

6

____

7

____

8

____

EXTRA PRACTICE 8

1. Write the missing words. 

doing • drawing • playing • reading • resting • running • studying • working • writing

Welcome to Kitty's blog!

Clau Souza/Arquivo da editora

Everybody is busy today.

Carol is ________________ English.

Jim and Leo are ________________ their homework.

Jim is ________________ a map for a Geography project

and Leo is ________________ the History book.

Liz and John are ________________ in the garden.

Uncle Steve is ________________ an e-mail and aunt

Susan is ________________ in the park.

Tobby is ________________ video game with his friends.

Only grandpa and grandma are ________________ at home.

2. Complete the crossword.

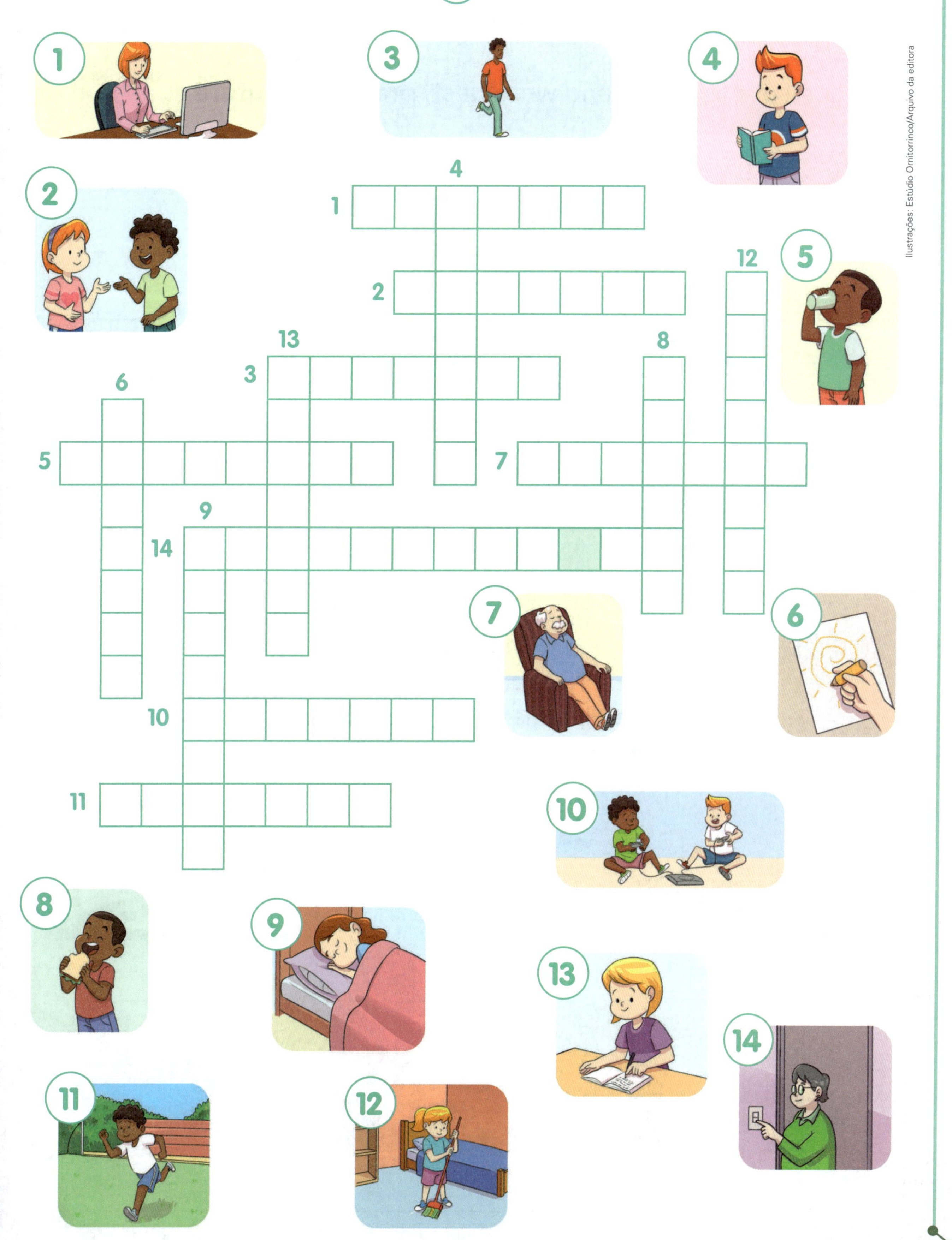

PROJECT 1 Kids tech life

1. Look at the poster and write **past, present** or **future**.  

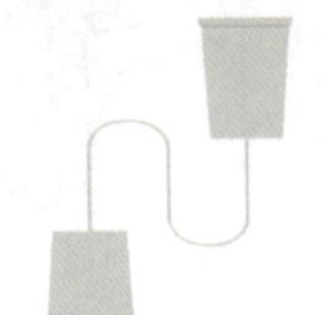

Smoke Signal
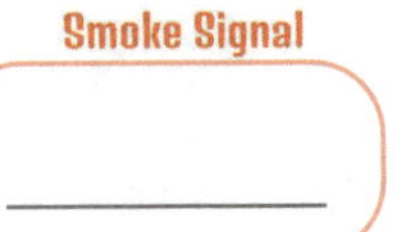
______

Carrier Pigeon
______

Telephone

______

Telephone

______

Mobile Phone
______

Video Call
______

3D Hologram
______

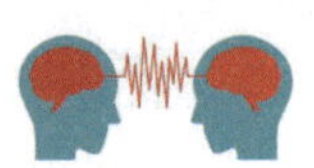
Telepathy
______

2. Label the pictures using the words from the box. 

smartphone • smartwatch • portable charger • tablet • drone • laptop

cristovao/Shutterstock
______

LDprod/Shutterstock
______

guteksk7/Shutterstock
______

StaceStock/Shutterstock
______

BT Image/Shutterstock
______

Dmitry Kalinovsky/Shutterstock
______

Shutterstock

3. Read the infographic and answer **T** (true) or **F** (false).  

SCREEN TIME
FACTS AND STATISTICS

1/3
One in three Internet users online worldwide is under 18 (UNICEF)

41% OF PARENTS
of 12-15s find it hard to control their child's screen time (OfCom)

53% OF CHILDREN
find it hard to control their own screen time (OfCom)

96% OF CHILDREN
spend more than 15 hours a week watching online content (Common Sense Media)

90% OF RESEARCH
on screen time in children found adverse associations between screen time and sleep health (Pediatrics)

Kids and Screens/Freepik

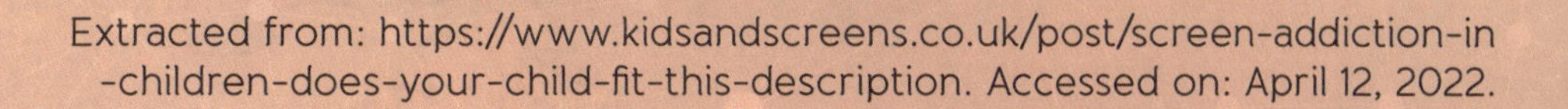
Extracted from: https://www.kidsandscreens.co.uk/post/screen-addiction-in-children-does-your-child-fit-this-description. Accessed on: April 12, 2022.

a) ◯ 41% of parents of 12-15s think it is not easy to control their child's screen time.

b) ◯ 96% of children spend more than 10 hours a week watching offline content.

c) ◯ One in three internet users online worldwide is under 18 (UNICEF).

d) ◯ 53% of adults find it hard to control their screen time.

e) ◯ All of research on screen time in children found adverse associations between screen time and sleep health.

4. Read the cartoons and talk to your classmates.  

Leandro Feliciano/Acervo do cartunista

"My teacher told me to read for an hour a day. Do Facebook and text messages count?"

© Randy Glasbergen/Acervo do cartunista

5. Read and answer the questions. Then interview a classmate and write the answers.

WHAT IS YOUR SCREEN TIME?

Burjan Zsolt/Shutterstock

	YOU		MY FRIEND ________	
DO YOU...	YES/NOT	HOW MANY HOURS PER WEEK?	YES/NOT	HOW MANY HOURS PER WEEK?
use a smartphone?				
use a tablet?				
play video game?				
play virtual reality games?				
watch TV series?				
use a computer?				
	TOTAL NUMBERS OF HOURS		TOTAL NUMBERS OF HOURS	

6. Let's create a screen time graph with the information from the group.

PROJECT 2 Our planet Earth

1. Read the text about Earth Day and circle the words related to nature.

History of Earth Day

Celebrate Earth Day with these tips for helping our environment.

DeVector/Shutterstock

Our planet is an amazing place, but it needs our help to thrive! That's why each year on April 22, more than a billion people celebrate Earth Day to protect the planet from things like pollution and deforestation. By taking part in activities like picking up litter and planting trees, we're making our world a happier, healthier place to live.

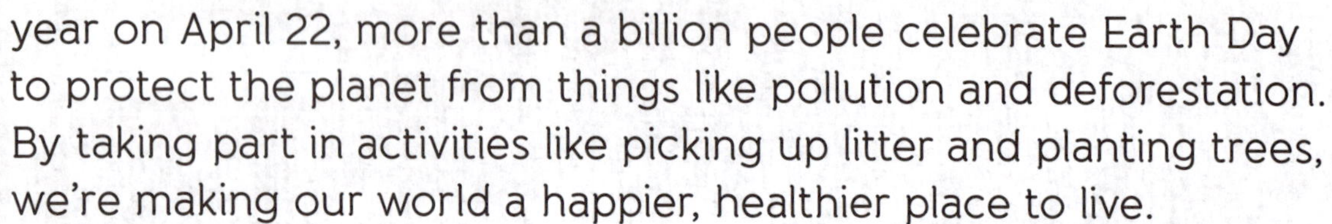

The first Earth Day was celebrated in 1970, when a United States senator from Wisconsin organized a national demonstration to raise awareness about environmental issues. [...] By 1990, Earth Day was an event celebrated by more than 140 countries around the globe. You can celebrate and protect the planet at the same time. [...]

tilialucida/Shutterstock

BE A PLANET HERO!

- In its lifetime, one reusable bag can prevent the use of 600 plastic bags.
- Recycling one can of soda, will save enough energy to power a TV for three hours.
- Shutting down a computer when it is not in use cuts the energy consumption by 85 percent.
- For every mile walked instead of driven, nearly one pound of pollution is keep out of the air.

Extracted from: https://kids.nationalgeographic.com/celebrations/article/earth-day. Accessed on: April 12, 2022.

2. Do you know the 3 R's? Read the text and complete the chart.

ABTA/Make Holidays Greener

water • sheets of paper • newspaper • fuel • clothes • energy • can of soda • broken glass bottle • cloth shopping bag

REDUCE	REUSE	RECYCLE

3. Answer the quiz.

How long does trash live?

a) Glass

- ( ) Millions
- ( ) 100 years

b) Plastic bottle

- ( ) 30 years
- ( ) 450 years

c) Aluminum cans

- ( ) 80-200 years
- ( ) 10-20 years

d) Paper

- ( ) 2-6 weeks
- ( ) 2-6 years

e) Plastic bag

- ( ) 200 years
- ( ) 10-1,000 years

f) Orange peel

- ( ) 6 months
- ( ) 2-5 weeks

g) Batteries

- ( ) 100 months
- ( ) 100 years

h) Milk carton

- ( ) 5 years
- ( ) 50 years

ZERO WASTE

Nina Fedorova/Shutterstock

Based on: https://www.dumpsters.com/blog/trash-life-cycle. Accessed on: April 12, 2022.

4. Read and answer the questions.  

What can you do to save the planet?

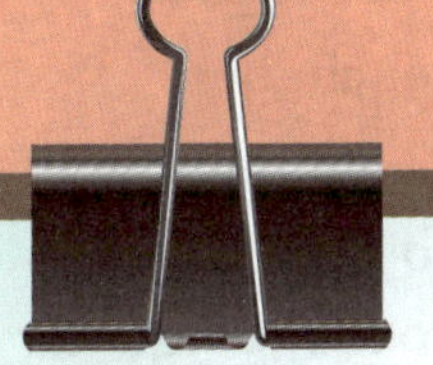

Banco de imagens/Arquivo da editora

a) What can you recycle?

____

____

b) What can you do around the house to conserve energy?

____

____

c) What do plants do for us and the Earth?

____

____

d) Why shouldn't we dump trash in the ocean?

____

____

e) What can we make from old or recyclable items?

____

____

5. Create a pocket guide with 5 actions that help us to save the Earth.

GLOSSARY

A

about: sobre; por volta de
accept: aceitar
according to: de acordo com
action: ação
act out: atuar; representar
add: adicionar; somar
address: endereço
adopted: adotado(a)
affect: afetar
afternoon: tarde
again: novamente
against: contra
age: idade
ahead: em frente
air conditioning: ar-condicionado
airplane: avião
all: todos
aloud: em voz alta
also: também
always: sempre
a.m.: antes do meio-dia (*ante meridiem*)
amazing: incrível
ancient: antigo
angry: irritado
answer: resposta; responder
ant: formiga
anxious: ansioso
anything: nada; algo
appear: parecem
apple: maçã
apple juice: suco de maçã
appliance: eletrodoméstico
April: abril
around: ao redor de; cerca de
arrival: chegada
arrive: chegar
Art room: sala de arte
as: como
ask: pedir; perguntar
at: no; na; para
author: autor
autumn: outono
average: média
awesome: legal; impressionante
axis: eixo

back: de volta; para trás
back spins: giros para trás
backward: para trás
bag: mala; mochila
baggie pants: calças tipo baggy
baggy pants: calças largas
balloon: bexiga; balão
barrel: barril
bash: festa
basket: cesta
bat: morcego
bath: banho de banheira
bathroom: banheiro
be: ser; estar
beat: batida musical
become: tornar-se
begin: iniciar, início
behind: atrás
best: o (a) melhor
be sure: ter certeza
better: melhor
between: entre
bill: conta
bin: lata de lixo
bird: pássaro
birthday: aniversário
biscuit: biscoito; bolacha
black: preto
blank: lacuna
blanket: cobertor
blessed: abençoado
blood vessels: vasos sanguíneos
bloom: florescer
blow out: apagar
blue: azul
board: lousa; tabuleiro
body: corpo
boost: impulso
bored: entediado
botanical: botânico
both: ambos
bottle: garrafa
bowl: tigela
box: caixa
bread: pão
breakfast: café da manhã
break time: intervalo; recreio
breathtaking: de tirar o fôlego
bright: brilhante
bring: trazer
broken: quebrado
brother: irmão
brown: marrom
brush: escovar
burn: queimar
but: mas
butterfly: borboleta
buy: comprar
by the way: a propósito

cafeteria: cantina
cake: bolo
call: chamar; telefonar
calves: músculo da panturrilha
campaign: campanha

can: pode; poder
candle: vela
candy: bala; guloseima
cap: boné; tampinha de garrafa
card: cartão
cardboard: papelão
carefully: cuidadosamente
carrot: cenoura
carrot cake: bolo de cenoura
cartoon: cartum; desenho animado
cat: gato
changes: mudanças
character: personagem
charger: carregador
check: ticar
checklist: lista
check (out): conferir
cheerleader: líder de torcida
chicken wrap: *wrap* de frango
child: criança; filho(a)
child-rearing: criação de filhos
children: crianças; filhos(as)
chips: batatas fritas
choose: escolher
circle: circular
citizen: cidadão
city: cidade
class: aula
classroom: sala de aula
clean: limpar
clock: relógio
close: fechar; perto
cloth: tecido
cloud: nuvem
coating: cobertura; revestimento
cocoa: cacau
cold: frio
color: cor; colorir
colorful: colorido
column: coluna
comb: pentear
come: vir
computer lab: laboratório de informática
Computer Science: Ciência da Computação
condiment: tempero
consumable: consumível
container: recipiente
contest: concurso
cook: cozinhar
cool: legal
cooler: caixa térmica
copy: copiar
correct: corrigir; correto
cost: custar
count: contar
countless: incontável
country: país
countryside: campo
create: criar
crisps: batatas fritas
cross: cruzar
crossword: palavras cruzadas
crowning: coroação
cry: chorar
cure: cura
curly: encaracolado
cute: fofo

D

dad: papai
daily: diário; diariamente
dark: escuro
date: data
day: dia
dear: querido(a)
deceive: enganar
December: dezembro
decompose: decompor
decorate: decorar
deliver: entregar
deny: negar
dinner: jantar
disease: doença
dish: prato
disorder: desordem
diversity: diversidade
divided: dividido
do: fazer
dog: cachorro
doll: boneca
donation: doação
don't: não (negação com verbo auxiliar)
down: para baixo
draw: desenhar
dress: vestido; vestir-se
drive: dirigir; passeio
drop off: deixar
drums: bateria
drumstick: baqueta
due to: devido a
dump: jogar

each: cada
early: cedo
Earth: Terra (planeta)
easy: fácil
eat: comer
effort: esforço
e-generation: geração tecnológica
elderly: idoso
endured: suportou
energy: energia
enjoy: divertir-se
enough: suficiente
environment: meio ambiente
essentials: itens básicos
evening: final de tarde; noite
every: cada; todo
everybody: todos
everyone: todos
everything: tudo
excuse: desculpar
expecting: esperando
exponentially: exponencialmente
express: expressar

F

fact: fato
fall: outono
fast: rápido
fat: gordo
father: pai
features: apresenta
February: fevereiro
feeling: sentimento
ferret: furão
fewer: menos
fill: preencher
find: achar; encontrar
fine: bem; bom (boa)
finger: dedo (da mão)
finger-friendly food: comida fácil de beliscar; petisco
firehouse: unidade do Corpo de Bombeiros
flag: bandeira
flashlight: lanterna
floor: chão; piso
flower: flor
folk art: arte folclórica
food: alimento
foot: pé
footwork: movimento, jogo de pés
for: para
forget: esquecer
forgive: perdoar
fork: garfo
free: livre
free-range eggs: ovos caipiras de granja
fresh: fresco; natural
Friday: sexta-feira
friend: amigo
friendship: amizade
from: de
fruit: fruta
fruit salad: salada de frutas
fun: diversão
funny: divertido; engraçado

G

garbage: lixo
garden: jardim
gardening: jardinagem
get rid of: livrar-se de algo
get up: levantar-se
get used to: acostumar-se
gift: presente
girl: menina
give: dar
glass: copo; vidro
glue: colar; cola
go: ir
good: bom (boa)
good-bye: tchau; até logo
good evening: boa noite
gosh: caramba; puxa vida
grandma: vovó
grandpa: vovô
grape: uva
great: grande; legal
greener holiday: férias ecológicas
greet: cumprimentar
grocery: mercearia
ground: chão; solo
grown: cresceu, crescido
grown-up: adulto
guess: adivinhar
guest: convidado
guitar: guitarra; violão
gym: ginásio esportivo

H

hair: cabelo
half: metade
hamstrings: isquiotibiais
hand: mão
handle: lidar com; cuidar de
handsome: bonito
handy: em mãos
happy: feliz
harm: fazer mal a; prejudicar
harvest: colheita
hat: chapéu
have: ter
head spins: giros de cabeça
health: saúde
healthy: saudável
hear: ouvir
heating: aquecedor
hello: olá; alô
help: ajuda; ajudar
helpful: prestativo (aquele que ajuda)
her: seu; dela
here: aqui
high-tech: de alta tecnologia
him: ele
his: seu; dele
hold: segurar
holiday: férias
home: lar; casa
homework: lição de casa
honesty: honestidade
hope: esperar
hopeful: esperançoso
hot: quente
house: casa
how: como
how much: quantos
hug: abraço
hungry: faminto

I

ice: gelo
if: se
illness: doença
in: em; dentro
include: incluir
induction: indução
in front of: em frente de
in line: em fila
in pairs: em pares; em duplas
insect: inseto
instead of: ao invés de
interesting: interessante
interview: entrevista
into: em

invitation: convite; convidar
invite: convite; convidar
issue: problema
it: ele; ela (animais e objetos)
its: seu; dele; dela (animais e objetos)

J

January: janeiro
job: emprego; trabalho
joke: piada; anedota
jolly: alegre
joy: alegria
juice: suco
July: julho
June: junho
just: apenas

keep: manter
key player: pessoa importante; essencial
kind: gentil; amável
kind of: tipo de
king: rei
kiss: beijo
knife: faca
know: saber
knowledge: conhecimento

L

land: terra; pousar
landfill: aterro sanitário
landscape: paisagem
language: língua; idioma
large: grande
largest: o maior
last: último; passado
later: depois
laugh: rir
learn: aprender
leave: deixar; sair
less: menos
let's: vamos
letter: letra; carta
library: biblioteca
life: vida
light: luz
like: gostar
listen: ouvir
litter: lixo
live: viver; morar
living room: sala de estar
long: longo; comprido
look: olhar; olhe
lots of: muitos; muitas
loud: alto
loved: amado
lovely: adorável
lunch: almoço
lung: pulmão
lyric: letra de música

M

made: feito
magazine: revista
make: fazer
man: homem
management: administração
man-made: artificial; feito pelo homem
manner: maneira
many: muitos
March: março
martial arts: artes marciais
mask: máscara
massive: maciço
match: associar
matter: problema; importar
May: maio
maybe: talvez
me: me; mim
meat: carne
meet: encontrar-se
message: mensagem
midday: meio-dia
midnight: meia-noite
milk: leite
milk carton: caixa de leite
mind: mente
mix: misturar
moist towelette: lenço umedecido
mom: mamãe
Monday: segunda-feira
month: mês
mood: astral, humor
more: mais
morning: manhã
most: o (a) mais
mother: mãe
move: mexer
moves: movimentos
movie: cinema
Mr.: sr. (senhor)
Ms.: sra. (senhora; senhorita)
music room: sala de música
must-have: algo que se deve ter
my: meu; minha
myself: eu mesmo(a)

napkin: guardanapo
narrower: mais estreito
nationality: nacionalidade
nature: natureza
near: próximo
need: necessitar; precisar
neighbor: vizinho
net: rede (na internet)
new: novo
newspaper: jornal
next: seguinte; próximo
next to: ao lado de
nice: bom; agradável
nighttime: noite; noturno
no: não
nobody: ninguém
noise: barulho
noon: meio-dia
not: não
note: anotação; bilhete
November: novembro
now: agora
number: número; numerar
nut: noz

O

obese: obeso
o'clock: hora exata; em ponto
October: outubro
odd: estranho; diferente
of: de
of course: é claro
office: escritório
oil: óleo; petróleo
old: velho
on: em; sobre
on foot: a pé
only: apenas; somente
open: abrir
or: ou
orange: laranja
orange juice: suco de laranja
other: outro
our: nosso(a)
out: fora
outdoor: fora de casa
outside: lado de fora
overnight: durante a noite
over there: lá
over time: ao longo do tempo
own: próprio

package: pacote; embalagem
packaging: embalagem
packing: arrumando (cesta ou mala)
page: página
pain: dor
paint: pintar
painted: pintado(a)
panel: painel
paper: papel
parent: o pai ou a mãe
participate: participar
party: festa
past: passado
pay: pagar
pen: caneta
pencil: lápis
people: pessoas
pepper: pimenta
permitted: permitido
per ton: por tonelada
phenomenon: fenômeno
photo: fotografia
Physical Education (P. E.): Educação Física
physical fitness: condicionamento físico
pick: pegar
picnic basket: cesta de piquenique
picture: figura; imagem; foto
pie: torta
piece of: pedaço de
pig: porco
place: lugar
plan: planejar
planet: planeta
plastic storage bag: sacola plástica
plate: prato
play: brincar; tocar
please: por favor
plus: sinal de adição; mais
p.m.: após o meio-dia (*post meridiem*)
polite: educado; polido
poor: pobre
portable: portátil
portrait: retrato
Portuguese: português
possible: possível
poster: cartaz
potato: batata
powder: pó
practice: praticar
preteen: pré-adolescente
pretty: bonito
probably: provavelmente
program: programa
put: colocar; pôr

Q

quads: quadríceps
quarter: quarto de hora; quinze minutos
queen: rainha
question: questão; pergunta
quick: rápido
quiet: quieto

rag: trapo
rainbow: arco-íris
read: ler
ready: pronto
really: realmente
receive: receber
rechargeable: recarregável
recipe: receita
recycle: reciclar
red: vermelho
refers: refere-se a
refillable: recarregável
relationships: relacionamentos
religion: religião
repair: consertar
required: requerido
research: pesquisa
resource: recurso
respect: respeitar; respeito
rest: descansar
return: voltar; retornar
reusable: reutilizável
revolve around: girar em torno de algo
rhythms: ritmos
ride: andar (de bicicleta)
right: certo; à direita
robot: robô
roll: enrolar
room: sala
root: raiz
rotate: girar
round: redondo; em torno de
routine: rotina
rubbish: lixo

run: correr
run away: fugir
runs: discorrer, acontecer

sacred: sagrado
sad: triste
safe: seguro
salt: sal
same: mesmo
Saturday: sábado
save: economizar
say: dizer
schedule: horário (escolar)
school: escola
schoolbag: mochila
Science: Ciências
science lab: laboratório de Ciências
Scotland: Escócia
screen: tela
sculpt: esculpir
sculptures: esculturas
search: procurar
seasons of the year: estações do ano
see: ver
send: enviar
senior: idoso
sentence: frase
September: setembro
set: aparelho
shade: sombra
shaking: sacudindo
sharp knife: faca afiada
she: ela
shine: brilhar
shop: fazer compras
short: baixo; curto
shower: banho; ducha
sick: doente
side: lado
sideways: na lateral, lateralmente
simple: simples
since: desde
sing: cantar
sister: irmã
sit down: sentar-se
sky: céu
slave: escravo(a)
sleep: dormir
smartwatch: relógio inteligente
smile: sorrir; sorriso
snake: cobra
sneakers: tênis
snow: neve
so: assim
soap: sabonete
soccer: futebol
Social Studies: Estudos Sociais
soda: refrigerante gasoso
solve: resolver
some: algum(ns)
someone: alguém
somersaults: cambalhotas
something: algo; alguma coisa
somewhere: em algum lugar
song: música
soon: logo; brevemente
sorry: desculpe(-me)
sound: som
sources: fontes
Spanish: espanhol
spare: disponível; livre
species: espécie
spend: gastar
spinach: espinafre
sponge: esponja
spoon: colher
spring: primavera
sprinkle: polvilhar; salpicar
staff: pessoal
stand up: levantar-se
stanzas: estrofes
start: começar
states: registros, estados
statue: estátua
stepfather: padrasto
stepmother: madrasta
stick: colar (adesivo)
still: ainda
stop: parar
straight: diretamente
straight ahead: direto, em frente
street: rua
strengthens: reforça
stuff: coisas
subject: assunto; disciplina escolar
substitute: substituto(a)
suffered: sofreu
suitcase: mala
suits: adequar-se
summer: verão
Sun: Sol
Sunday: domingo
sunglasses: óculos escuros
sunscreen: protetor solar
sure: certo; certamente
surf: navegar
surprised: surpreso(a)
sweat: suor
sweetie: docinho; querido
sweets: doces
swim: nadar
swimming pool: piscina
switch/off: apagar; desligar
switch/on: acender; ligar

table: mesa
tablecloth: toalha de mesa
tablespoon: colher de sopa
take: tomar; pegar
take notes: tomar notas; anotar
talk: falar
tall: alto(a)
tap: torneira
teacher: professor(a)
tear: lágrima
tech: tecnologia
teenager: adolescente
teeth: dentes

than: do que
thanks: obrigado(a)
thank you: obrigado(a)
that: aquele; aquela; aquilo; esse; essa; isso
the: o; a; os; as
their: deles; delas
them: os; as (pronome)
theme: tema
then: então; depois
there: lá
there are: há; existem
there is: há; existe
these: estes; estas
they: eles; elas
thin: magro
thing: coisa
this: este; esta; isto
those: aqueles; aquelas; esses; essas
through: através
throw: atirar; jogar
throw away: jogar algo fora
thumb: polegar
Thursday: quinta-feira
time: tempo; hora
tired: cansado
to: para
today: hoje
together: junto
toiletry: produtos de higiene pessoal
tonight: à noite
touchable: palpável
Tourette's syndrome: síndrome de Tourette
towel: toalha
town: cidade
trash: lixo
trash bag: saco de lixo
trash can: lata de lixo
travel: viajar
tree: árvore
trick: travessura
true: verdadeiro
try: tentar
Tuesday: terça-feira
tuna: atum
turn: vez
turn off: desligar
turn on: ligar
twice: duas vezes

ugly: feio(a)
under: sob; embaixo de
understand: entender
unhappy: infeliz
unplug: desligar
unscramble: desembaralhar
until: até
up: para cima
upcoming: próximos
use: usar
used to be: costumava ser
usually: geralmente

vegetable: vegetal; verdura
version: versão
very: muito
very good: muito bem

wait: esperar
wake up: despertar; acordar
walk: caminhar; passear
want: querer
warm: aquecer
was: foi; era; estava
wash: lavar
waste: desperdiçar; desperdício
watch: observar; assistir
water: água
watermelon: melancia
way: caminho; jeito; modo
we: nós
wear: vestir
web: teia; rede (internet)
Wednesday: quarta-feira
week: semana
weekend: fim de semana
weekly: semanal
welcome: bem-vindo
well: bem
what: que; qual
What about...?: Que tal...?
wheelchair: cadeira de rodas
when: quando
where: onde
which: que; qual
while: enquanto
white: branco
who: quem
why: por que
window: janela
winter: inverno
wise: inteligente; sábio
with: com
without: sem
woman: mulher
wonderful: maravilhoso
word: palavra
work: trabalhar
worker: trabalhador
world: mundo
worn: desgastado
worry: preocupar
wrist: pulso
wristband: pulseira
write: escrever

year: ano
yellow: amarelo
you: você(s)
your: seu(s); sua(s)
yourself: se; a si mesmo

STRUCTURES

EM INGLÊS DIZEMOS:	PARA DIZER:
When is the History class?	Quando é a aula de História?
It's on Friday.	É na sexta-feira.
What's the first day of the week?	Qual é o primeiro dia da semana?
Sunday is the first day of the week.	Domingo é o primeiro dia da semana.
What do you do at seven a.m.?	O que você faz às sete horas da manhã?
I get up.	Eu me levanto.
Why are you sad?	Por que você está triste?
I'm sad because I can't play the guitar.	Estou triste porque não posso/sei tocar violão.
I can't do my homework.	Eu não consigo fazer minha lição de casa.
Can you swim?	Você sabe/pode nadar?
Yes, I can. / No, I can't.	Sim, eu sei/posso. / Não, eu não sei/ não posso.
Can I help you?	Eu posso te ajudar?
Yes, please.	Sim, por favor.
Is she a child?	Ela é uma criança?
No, she isn't. She is a teenager.	Não, não é. Ela é uma adolescente.
How many students are there in the classroom?	Quantos alunos há na sala de aula?
There are thirty students.	Há trinta alunos.

EM INGLÊS DIZEMOS:	PARA DIZER:
Where are you?	Onde você está?
I'm at school.	Estou na escola.
What's your address?	Qual é o seu endereço?
My address is 28, Ford Street.	Meu endereço é 28 Ford Street.
How old are you?	Quantos anos você tem?
I'm ten years old.	Eu tenho dez anos.
When is your birthday?	Quando é seu aniversário?
It's on February 16th.	É no dia 16 de fevereiro.
What time is it?	Que horas são?
It's four o'clock.	São quatro horas.
What's your job?	Qual é a sua profissão?
I'm a dentist.	Eu sou dentista.
Are these flowers red?	Estas flores são vermelhas?
No, they aren't. These flowers are yellow.	Não, não são. Estas flores são amarelas.
Where are you from?	De onde você é?
I am from Brazil.	Eu sou do Brasil.
What's your nationality?	Qual é a sua nacionalidade?
I am Brazilian.	Eu sou brasileiro(a).
What languages do you speak?	Quais línguas você fala?
I speak Portuguese and English.	Eu falo português e inglês.
What's Jim doing?	O que Jim está fazendo?
He is reading a book.	Ele está lendo um livro.

UNIT 1

WHAT'S YOUR FAVORITE SUBJECT?

Name: ____________________

Class: ____________________ **Date:** ___/___/___

1. Look, read and complete.  

a) I'm Anika. I love experiments! My favorite subject is __________ and my favorite place at school is the __________!

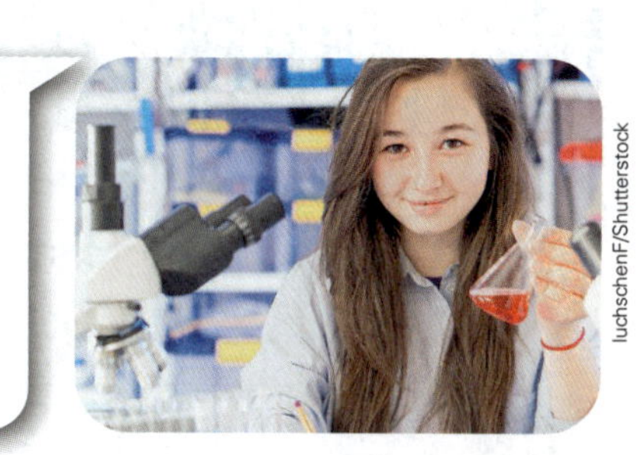
IuchschenF/Shutterstock

b) I'm Jeff. I love painting! My favorite subject is __________ and my favorite place at school is the __________!

Monkey Business Images/Shutterstock

c) I'm Dan. I love calculations! My favorite subject is __________ __________!

vectorfusionart/Shutterstock

d) I'm Rachel. I love sports! ____________________ ____________________!

Sergey Novikov/Shutterstock

WORKBOOK

2. Look at the picture and answer. 

Estúdio Ornitorrinco/Arquivo da editora

a) How many History books are there in the classroom?

____

b) Are there English books in the classroom?

____

c) What time is the Social Studies class?

____

d) What day is today?

____

3. Count and write the numbers.  

a) Seventy plus a hundred and thirty equals two hundred.

b) One thousand minus one hundred equals ______________.

c) Seventy divided by ten equals ______________.

d) Three hundred times two equals ______________.

e) Seven hundred plus sixty-four equals ______________.

UNIT 2

ARE YOU READY?

Name: ______________________________

Class: ____________________ **Date:** ___/___/___

1. Read the text messages and number the pictures.  

Artem Mashchenko/Shutterstock

Ilustrações: Estúdio Ornitorrinco/Arquivo da editora

WORKBOOK

2. Read and match. 

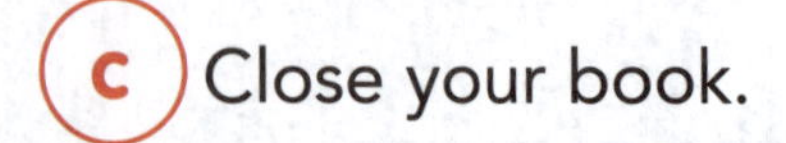

a Silence, please!

b Stand up!

c Close your book.

d It's time to get up!

Andrey_Popov/Shutterstock

photobyphotoboy/Shutterstock

wavebreakmedia/Shutterstock

Prostock-studio/Shutterstock

3. Complete the dialog and check the matching comic strip.  

because • bakery • breakfast • everything • hi • school • what

Emmy: Hi, Miguel! Is ____________ OK?

Miguel: ____________, Emmy. I'm not OK.

Emmy: Why not?

Miguel: ____________ I'm late for ____________. You are late too!

Emmy: No, we are not!

Miguel: ____________ time is it?

Emmy: It is six thirty!

Miguel: Really?

Emmy: We are not late, Miguel! Let's have ____________ at the ____________?

Miguel: Yes, let's go.

Ilustrações: Estúdio Ornitorrinco/Arquivo da editora

WORKBOOK

UNIT 3

CAN YOU PLAY THE DRUMS?

Name: ______________________________

Class: ____________________ **Date:** ___ / ___ / ___

1. Match the sentences to the pictures. Then write full sentences.

a) Daniel can	( ) love gardening.
b) Monica and her mother	( ) play the drums well.
c) Jill can	( ) upset with the students.
d) The teacher is	( ) play the guitar.

____

____

____

____

Szasz-Fabian Ilka Erika/Shutterstock

Monkey Business Images/Shutterstock

adriaticfoto/Shutterstock

TimeImage Production/Shutterstock

WORKBOOK

2. Read and complete.

How are the kids feeling today?

Paul is feeling ______________.

Camile is ______________

______________.

Patty ______________

______________.

FAMILY
GRANDPA
How are you feeling today, kids?
PAUL
I'm
CAMILE
I'm
PATTY
I'm

3. Look and complete. Then draw what you can and can't do.

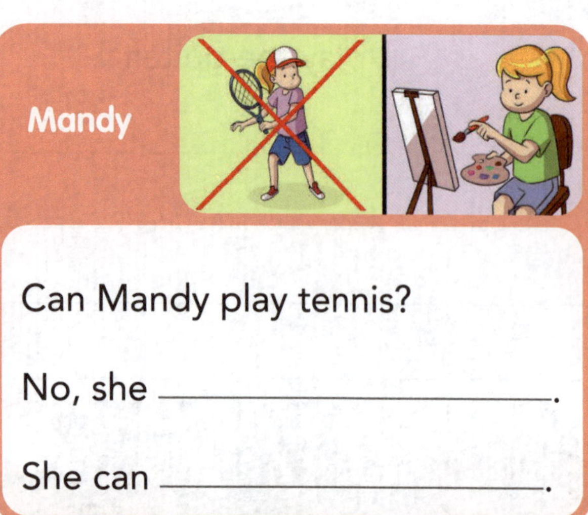

Can Mandy play tennis?

No, she ______________.

She can ______________.

Can Kevin ______________?

No, ______________. He

______________.

Can ______________?

No, ______________.

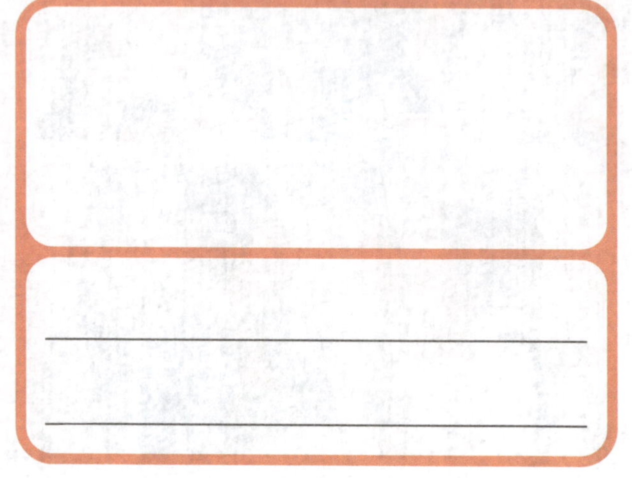

____

____

Ilustrações: Estúdio Ornitorrinco/Arquivo da editora

WORKBOOK

UNIT 4

THE E-GENERATION

Name: ______________________________

Class: ______________________ **Date:** ___/___/___

1. Unscramble and complete the sentences. 

a) 
Monkey Business Images/Shutterstock

a – she – grown-up – is?

____

__________, she isn't. She __________ a preteen girl.

b) 
Diego Cervo/Shutterstock

elderly – they – are?

____

Yes, ______________________.

c) 
Monkey Business Images/Shutterstock

is – a – child – she?

____

______________________. She is a

______________________ woman.

d) 
oliveromg/Shutterstock

they – are – babies?

____

______________________. They

are ______________________.

WORKBOOK

2. Complete the sentences gaps. 

a car • the bills online • on the cell phone • on the Internet every day • homework • to good music • to parties with friends • video game with my brother

a) I play ______________________________.

b) My grandparents chat ______________________________.

c) I usually go ______________________________.

d) I like to listen ______________________________.

e) My parents pay ______________________________.

f) I can't drive ______________________________.

g) I usually do the ______________________________.

h) They talk a lot ______________________________.

3. Read the questions and check.

a) What do you do when you are a baby?

◯ Play video game.

◯ Eat, cry and sleep.

b) What do you do when you are a grown-up?

◯ Go to work and pay bills.

◯ Cry and draw.

c) What do you do when you are a preteen?

◯ Pay bills.

◯ Do homework and chat on the Internet.

d) What do you do when you are a child?

◯ Drive a car.

◯ Play video games and do homework.

UNIT 5 NATURE AND PICNIC

Name: ______________________________

Class: ____________________ **Date:** ___/___/___

1. Look and write. For the picnic...

Ilustrações: Ilustra Cartoon/Arquivo da editora

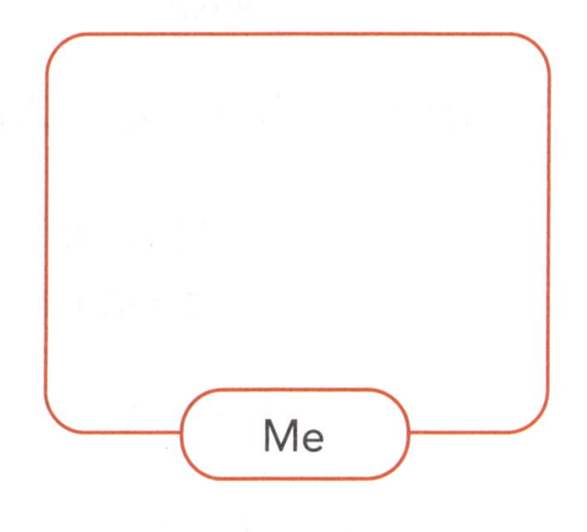

a) Tom has ______________________________.

b) Melinda and Melanie have ______________________________.

c) Christine has ______________________________.

d) Akio has ______________________________.

e) Paula has ______________________________.

f) I have ______________________________.

WORKBOOK

2. Write the sentences in the plural form.

a) This is my fork.

____

b) That is the picnic plate.

____

c) There is one girl in the swimming pool.

____

3. Complete the dialog and check the pictures.

hot • season • spring • summer • winter

Janice: What is your favorite ______________, Melissa?

Melissa: Well, I prefer ______________.

Janice: Summer? Why?

Melissa: Because summer is ______________ and I can go to the beach.

Janice: How about winter?

Melissa: I like ______________ too because we can drink hot chocolate, but my favorite season is summer! How about you?

Janice: I like fall, but my favorite season is ______________ because I love flowers!

Krakenimages.com/Shutterstock

( ) Melissa
( ) Janice

KidStock/Blend Images/Getty Images

( ) Melissa
( ) Janice

WORKBOOK

UNIT 6

A BIRTHDAY PARTY

Name: ______________________

Class: ______________________ **Date:** ____ / ____ / ____

1. Complete the dialog. Write Mandy's birthday invitation card. 

How • What time • When • Where

Mandy: Hi, Louise.

Louise: Hi, Mandy! ______________ are you?

Mandy: I'm fine, thanks. Can you come to my birthday party?

Louise: Sure! ______________ is it?

Mandy: It is on August 22nd.

Louise: ______________ is the party?

Mandy: It is at 6 p.m.

Louise: ______________ is the party?

Mandy: It is at 334, New Castle Avenue. We will have pizza, sweets, hamburgers, ice cream and chocolate cake!

Louise: I love pizza! But I love you more!

Lifesummerlin/Shutterstock

WORKBOOK

2. Look and complete the sentences.

Drazen Zigic/ Shutterstock

1 Sam • sixth month • eighth day

Kolpakova Daria/ Shutterstock

2 Melissa • first month • twentieth day

Halfpoint/ Shutterstock

3 John • third month • first day

Studio Romantic/ Shutterstock

4 Martina • tenth month • second day

a) Sam is the ___first child___. Sam's birthday is ___on June 8th___.

b) Melissa is the ____________. Melissa's birthday is ____________.

c) John is the ____________. John's ____________.

d) Martina ____________.

3. Complete the sequence.

a) third, thirteenth, ____________

b) second, sixth, ____________, fourteenth

c) ninth, eighth, seventh, ____________

d) ____________, eleventh, twenty-first, thirty-first

e) fifth, tenth, ____________, twentieth, ____________

WORKBOOK

UNIT 7 A CULTURAL FAIR

Name: ______________________

Class: ______________ Date: ___/___/___

1. Look and write. 

a) 

Monkey Business Images/Shutterstock

Annika / Cape Town, South Africa

My name is Annika. I'm from Cape Town, South Africa. I am South African and I speak English.

b) 

Andy Dean Photography/Shutterstock

Juan Carlos / Cancun, Mexico

____
____
____

c) 

John Roman Images/Shutterstock

Emilio / Rome, Italy

____
____
____

d) 

Monkey Business Images/Shutterstock

Huang / Pequin, China

____
____
____

2. Answer.

Australian • blue, white and red • English • Perth, Australia • surfing

a) Where are you from? I'm from ______________________.

b) What's your nationality? I'm ______________________.

c) What's your favorite sport? My favorite sport is ______________________.

d) What language do you speak? I speak ______________________.

e) What are the colors of the Australian flag? They are ______________________.

3. Look and circle the correct words. 

Serhii Yevdokymov/Shutterstock

a) The United Kingdom flag is under / on the shelf.

Lenka Venska/Shutterstock

b) The white dog is under / between the chair.

Cecilia Di Dio/Shutterstock

c) The Argentinian alfajors are between / in the box.

Tanee/Shutterstock

d) The English tea box is behind / on the tea cup and the honey.

UNIT 8 YOU CAN HELP THE PLANET

Name: ______________________________

Class: ____________________ **Date:** ____ / ____ / ____

1. Look and circle the correct word.

a) Garfield is *hungry / thirsty*.

b) There is a *cat / human* hair in his plate.

c) Garfield is *eating / drinking* cat food.

2. Unscramble, write the sentences and match.  

a) is – switching off – Daniel – the – TV – .

____

____

Igor Emmerich/Cultura Exclusive/Getty Images

b) video game – Mark and his friends – playing – are – .

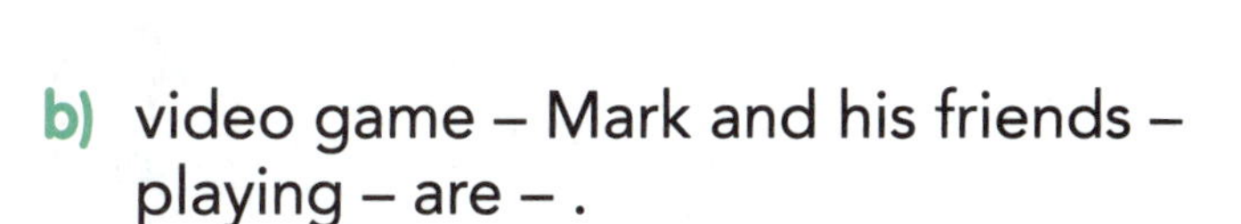

____

____

Rawpixel.com/Shutterstock

c) to – running – James – is – school – .

____

____

George Rudy/Shutterstock

WORKBOOK

3. Look at the pictures and complete. 

a) **Mom:** What _are you doing_, Matt? **(do)**

Matt: I _am washing_ my hands, mom. **(wash)**

Mom: Do not waste water, OK?

Matt: OK, mom!

Pikul Noorod/Shutterstock

b) **Sandy:** What ________ those people ________? **(do)**

Tom: They are volunteers. They ________ the public park. **(clean)**

Rawpixel.com/Shutterstock

c) **Jim:** ________ Jillian ________? **(watch)**

Grandma: No, she isn't.

Jim: What ________ she ________? **(do)**

Grandma: She ________ the dog. **(walk)**

Dean Drobot/Shutterstock

d) **Mary:** ________ the babies ________ milk? **(drink)**

Stella: No, Joshua ________ milk and Joseph is ________. **(drink/eat)**

Mary: What ________ their father ________? **(do)**

Stella: He ________ the garage. **(clean)**

John-Alex/Shutterstock

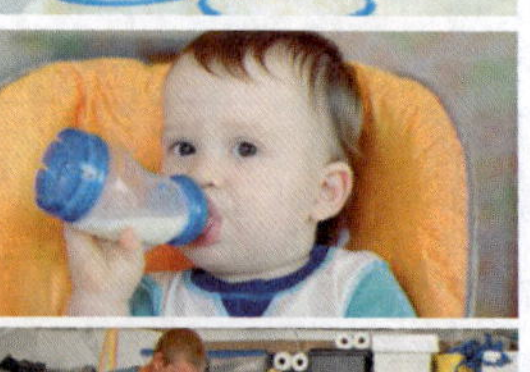

Ivolodina/Shutterstock

Trekandshoot/Glenda M. Powers/Shutterstock

CELEBRATION CRAFTS

Happy Easter!

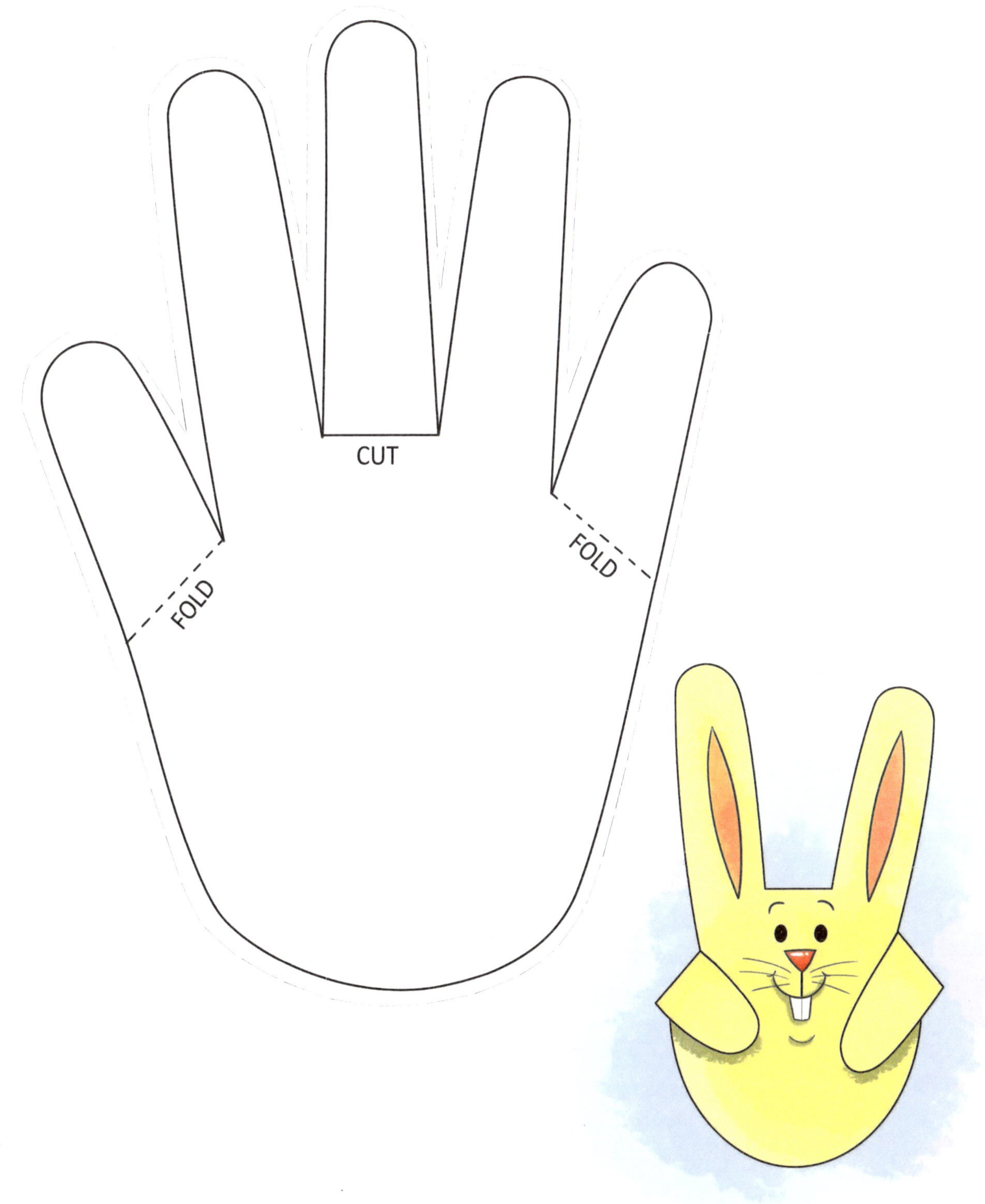

Ilustra Cartoon/Arquivo da editora

Happy Friendship Day!

Happy Mother's Day!

Ilustrações: Ilustra Cartoon/Arquivo da editora

Happy Father's Day!

Happy Thanksgiving Day!

Ilustra Cartoon/Arquivo da editora

I'm thankful for...

Merry Christmas and Happy New Year!

Ilustrações: Ilustra Cartoon/Arquivo da editora

MINI CARDS

Instruções

- O envelope e as minicartas devem ser destacados com cuidado.
- Depois de destacado da folha, o envelope deve ser dobrado e colado nos locais indicados. Nele serão guardadas as minicartas.

——— dobre
-------- destaque

HELLO! KIDS 5

HELLO! KIDS 5

GLUE

GLUE

Clau Souza/Arquivo da editora
Marcos Mello/Arquivo da editora

MINI CARDS

Material integrante da Coleção **Hello! Kids 5**
Eliete Canesi Morino • Rita Brugin de Faria
Reprodução e venda proibidas

editora ática

NAME:

SPRING	SUMMER	FALL	WINTER	AUSTRALIA
BRAZIL	CANADA	CHINA	ENGLAND	INDIA
JAPAN	NEW ZEALAND	PORTUGAL	RUSSIA	SOUTH AFRICA
THE UNITED STATES OF AMERICA	SPINACH PIE	SANDWICH	SWEETS	CAKE
WATERMELON	COOKIES	ORANGE JUICE	TALL MAN	SHORT MAN
FAT DOG	THIN DOG	UGLY FACE	PRETTY FACE	NEW CAR

Ilustrações: Ilustra Cartoon/Arquivo da editora

STICKERS

Name: ______________________

Class: ______________________

Name: ______________________

Class: ______________________

Page 11

B Brown/Shutterstock

Monkey Business Images/Shutterstock

PotatoTomato/Shutterstock

Slavica/iStockphoto/Getty Images

Rade Kovac/Shutterstock

Naumenko Aleksandr/Shutterstock

Stockfour/Shutterstock

didon/Shutterstock

Gorodenkoff/Shutterstock

Pages 8 and 9

Pages 22 and 23

Pages 38 and 39

Page 25

Ilustrações: Ilustra Cartoon/Arquivo da editora

Page 41

Nejron Photo/Shutterstock

Ksenia Vorobeva/Shutterstock

Kiselev Andrey Valerevich/Shutterstock

Magomed Magomedagaev/Shutterstock

Duplass/Shutterstock

Oliver Hoffmann/Shutterstock

Samuel Borges Photography/Shutterstock

Viacheslav Nikolaenko/Shutterstock

Yakobchuk Viacheslav/Shutterstock

Pages 52 and 53

Marcos Mello/Arquivo da editora

Pages 68 and 69

Marcos Mello/Arquivo da editora

Page 55

MaLija/Shutterstock

Makistock/Shutterstock

Ollyy/Shutterstock

Studio Romantic/Shutterstock

michaeljung/Shutterstock

wavebreakmedia/Shutterstock

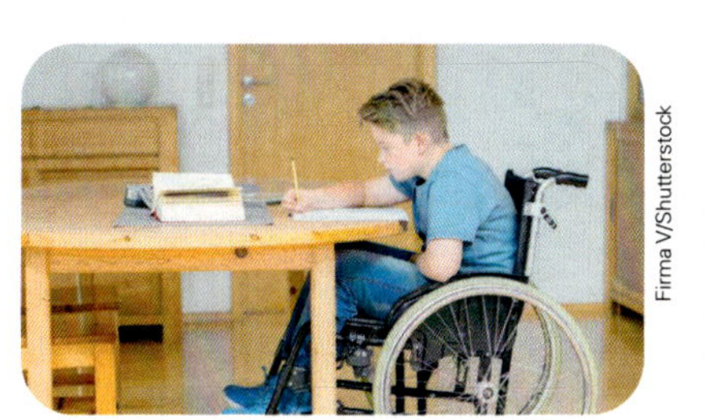
Firma V/Shutterstock

RHJPhtotos/Shutterstock

Kaspars Grinvalds/Shutterstock

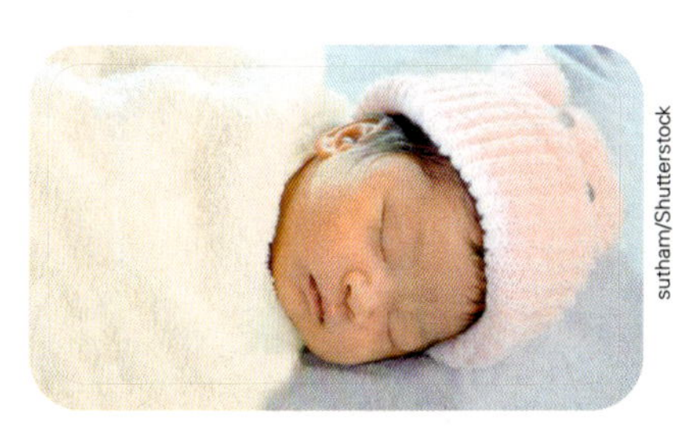
sutham/Shutterstock

Rido/Shutterstock

WAYHOME studio/Shutterstock

Page 71

J.Dream/Shutterstock

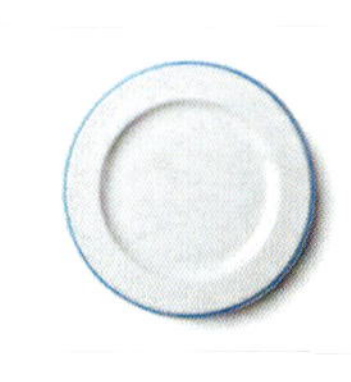

Suradech Prapairat/ Shutterstock

GMEVIPHOTO/ Shutterstock

azure1/Shutterstock

Preto Perola/ Shutterstock

AGorohov/Shutterstock

Amnaj Tandee/ Shutterstock

Moving Moment/ Shutterstock

Alexander Raths/ Shutterstock

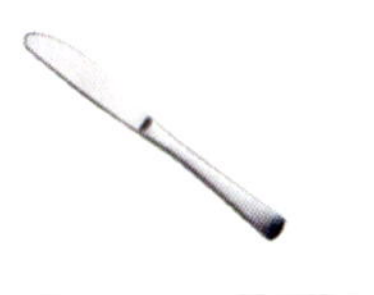
kiboka/Shutterstock

Garsya/Shutterstock

JIANG HONGYAN/ Shutterstock

Nixx Photography/ Shutterstock

Valentina Proskurina/ Shutterstock

Aprilphoto/Shutterstock

ffolas/Shutterstock

Page 73

Soloviova Liudmyla/Shutterstock

Sunny studio/Shutterstock

Mira Arnaudova/Shutterstock

majatoni/Shutterstock

Page 85

Africa Studio/Shutterstock

gpointstudio/Shutterstock

Lopolo/Shutterstock

Arina P Habich/Shutterstock

Alhovik/Shutterstock

Dobryak839/Shutterstock

CKA/Shutterstock

Iakov Filimonov/Shutterstock

Javier Brosch/Shutterstock

sirtravelalot/Shutterstock

Syda Productions/Shutterstock

Visual Intermezzo/Shutterstock

Page 101

Bandeira da Inglaterra: Julinzy/Shutterstock; demais bandeiras: Banco de imagens/Arquivo da editora

Pages 82 and 83

Marcos Mello/Arquivo da editora

Pages 98 and 99

Marcos Mello/Arquivo da editora

Pages 112 and 113

Marcos Mello/Arquivo da editora

Page 115

LightField Studios/Shutterstock

Phat1978/Shutterstock

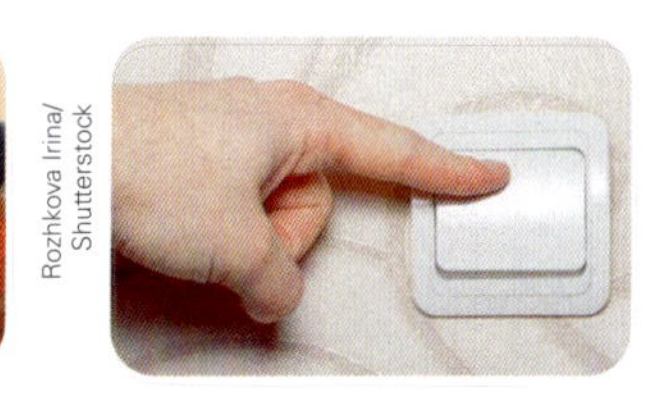
Rozhkova Irina/Shutterstock

Andrey_Popov/Shutterstock

Cultura Motion/Shutterstock

Africa Studio/Shutterstock

HSSphoto/Shutterstock

Mladen Zivkovic/Shutterstock

Irelee/Shutterstock

skyNext/Shutterstock

CreativeZone/Shutterstock

LumineImages/Shutterstock

India Picture/Shutterstock

Ivica Drusany/Shutterstock

Mila Supinskaya Glashchenko/Shutterstock

Milanzeremski/Shutterstock

Jomkanok Jiraboonyayanon/Shutterstock

Prostock-studio/Shutterstock

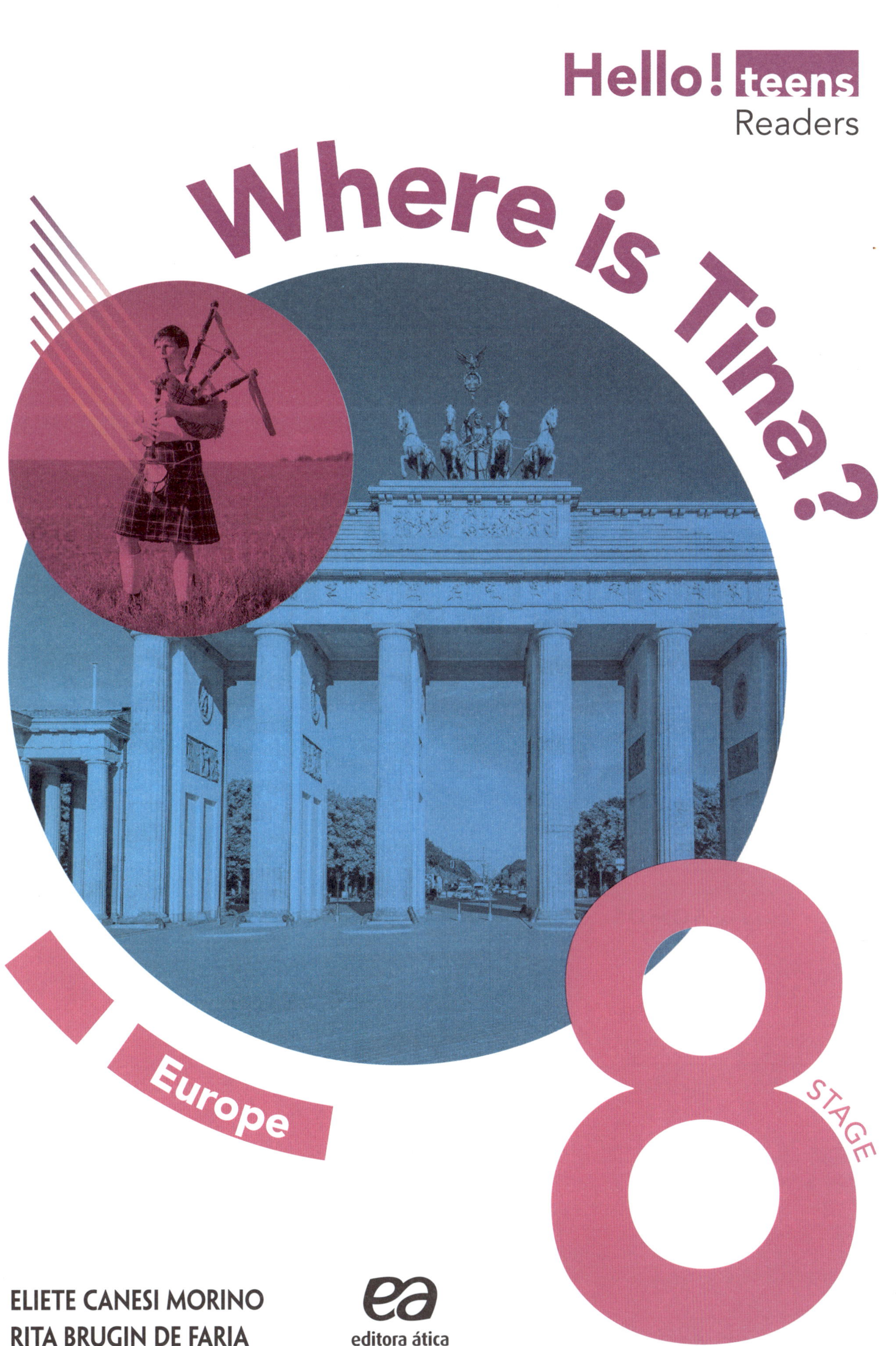
Hello! teens
Readers
Where is Tina?
Europe
8
STAGE
ELIETE CANESI MORINO
RITA BRUGIN DE FARIA
ea
editora ática

Direção Presidência: Mario Ghio Júnior

Direção de Conteúdo e Operações: Wilson Troque

Direção editorial: Luiz Tonolli e Lidiane Vivaldini Olo

Gestão de projeto editorial: Mirian Senra

Gestão de área: Alice Silvestre

Coordenação: Renato Malkov

Edição: Ana Lucia Militello, Carla Fernanda Nascimento (assist.), Caroline Santos, Danuza Dias Gonçalves, Maiza Prande Bernardello, Milena Rocha (assist.), Sabrina Cairo Bileski

Planejamento e controle de produção: Patrícia Eiras e Adjane Queiroz

Revisão: Hélia de Jesus Gonsaga (ger.), Kátia Scaff Marques (coord.), Rosângela Muricy (coord.), Ana Curci, Ana Paula C. Malfa, Arali Gomes, Brenda T. M. Morais, Diego Carbone, Gabriela M. Andrade, Luís M. Boa Nova, Patricia Cordeiro, Paula T. de Jesus, Ricardo Miyake; Amanda T. Silva e Bárbara de M. Genereze (estagiárias)

Arte: Daniela Amaral (ger.), Catherine Saori Ishihara (coord.) e Letícia Lavôr (edit. arte)

Diagramação: Mariana Munhato

Iconografia e tratamento de imagem: Sílvio Kligin (ger.), Claudia Bertolazzi (coord.), Mariana Valeiro (pesquisa iconográfica), Cesar Wolf e Fernanda Crevin (tratamento)

Licenciamento de conteúdos de terceiros: Thiago Fontana (coord.), Flavia Zambon e Angra Marques (licenciamento de textos), Erika Ramires, Luciana Pedrosa Bierbauer, Luciana Cardoso Sousa e Claudia Rodrigues (analistas adm.)

Ilustrações: Igor RAS

Cartografia: Eric Fuzii (coord.), Robson Rosendo da Rocha (edit. arte)

Design: Gláucia Koller (ger.), Talita Guedes (proj. gráfico), Luis Vassallo (capa) e Gustavo Vanini (assist. arte)

Foto de capa: Patryk Kosmider/Shutterstock e GRSI/Shutterstock

---

Avenida das Nações Unidas, 7221, 3º andar, Setor A
Pinheiros – São Paulo – SP – CEP 05425-902
Tel.: 4003-3061
www.atica.com.br / editora@atica.com.br

2024
Código da obra 742204
OP: 251061 (AL)
1ª impressão
1ª edição
De acordo com a BNCC.

Impressão acabamento: EGB Editora Gráfica Bernardi

Hello!
Would you like to travel with me again?
This time I will experience some fun situations in several countries in Europe. Come on! Let's discover facts and curiosities about these countries together!
EUROPE
Igor RAS/Arquivo da editora

#DAY1

LONDON, ENGLAND

Is There a Safe?

Tina: Please, sir! Are there any messages for me?

Receptionist: No, there aren't.

Tina: Can I lock my passport and money in the safe?

Receptionist: Yes, sure! There is a leaflet with instructions to program the safe's password in your room.

Tina: Oh! One more question… I need to exchange some dollars into pounds. Is there an exchange house nearby?

Receptionist: Yes, there is. It's next to the underground station on Oxford Street.

Tina: Great! Thank you!

Igor RAS/Arquivo da editora

England

Capital: London
Location: Nothern Europe
Area: 130,395 sq. km
Population: 55,619,400
Currency: Pound Sterling
Language: English
Nationality: English

Mapa e bandeira: Banco de imagens/Arquivo da editora

CROSS CULTURAL

The London Eye, a 135-meter-tall Ferris wheel, was built on the banks of the River Thames and inaugurated on December 31, 1999. The London Eye is one of London's most famous landmarks and it is considered to be a symbol as important as the Eiffel Tower in Paris.

mkos83/Shutterstock

THE LONDON EYE.

1 Read and complete the text.

The London Eye is a ____________________ located in the heart of ____________________. Its importance to the city is comparable to the ____________________ in Paris.

2 Fill in the blanks with information about your city.

The most important landmark of my city is ____________________. It is ____________________ and it was built in ____________________.

3 Read the text about The Beatles and answer the questions.

Mirrorpix/Getty Images

The Beatles is one of the most famous bands in the world. Its four members, George Harrison, John Lennon, Paul McCartney and Ringo Starr, were born in Liverpool, England. Their songs still make a big success around the world. Paul McCartney announced the end of the group in 1970 and its members began solo careers.

THE BEATLES PLAYING ON A TV SHOW, 1964.

a. Where were the members of The Beatles born?

____

b. When did The Beatles end?

____

c. Do some research and write the name of four songs from The Beatles.

____

____

#DAY48

EDINBURGH, SCOTLAND

Where Is the Bus Stop?

Tina: Excuse me, sir. Where is the nearest Big Red Bus Stop?

Man: You have to walk two blocks that way.

Tina: Thank you.

Man: Can you see that red sign there? That's the bus stop.

Tina: Yes, sure. By the way, do you know if the bus goes to Edinburgh Castle?

Man: Hmmm! I think it goes, but you'd better check. You can ask for "The Big Bus" pamphlet at the bus stop.

Tina: Thanks, sir.

Man: You're welcome.

Igor RAS/Arquivo da editora

Scotland

Capital: Edinburgh
Location: Northern Europe
Area: 77,933 sq. km
Population: 5,424,800
Currency: Pound Sterling
Languages: English, Scottish Gaelic, Scots
Nationality: Scottish

Mapa e bandeira: Banco de imagens/ Arquivo da editora

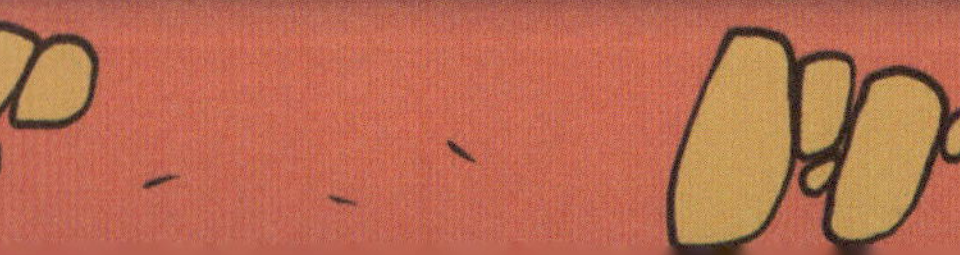

The kilt is one of the most famous national costumes in the world. It's certainly what people associate with Scotland, along with the bagpipes. Some people consider very bad luck to wear a kilt in a tartan that does not belong to your family. If you visit Scotland, just remind that men do not wear skirts, they wear kilts.

GRSI/Shutterstock

A SCOTTISH MAN PLAYING THE BAGPIPES.

1 Answer the questions.

a. What is Scotland associated with?

____

b. When is it bad luck to wear a kilt?

____

2 Write **T** (True) or **F** (False) according to the dialog.

a. ( ) Tina is far away from the bus stop.

b. ( ) The man is giving Tina some information.

c. ( ) The man said that it was not necessary to check the information about the bus.

3 Read the text below.

LOCH NESS "MONSTER"

The Loch Ness "monster" – affectionately known as "Nessie" – is a supposed plesiosaur-like creature living in Loch Ness, a long and deep lake in Scotland.

The modern legend of Nessie begins in 1934 with Dr. Robert Kenneth Wilson, a physician who supposedly photographed a plesiosaur-like beast with a long neck emerging out of the dark waters. Before the photo, Loch Ness was the stuff of legend and myth, but people came to the lake more to relax than to go on expeditions looking for mythical beasts. After the photo, the scientific experts were called in. First, they examined the photo itself. It could be a plesiosaur, but it could be a tree trunk too. Later, there would be explorations by a submarine with high tech sensing devices. Today, we have a tourist industry with boat and submarine rides and a multimedia tourist center.

Based on: <www.skepdic.com/nessie.html>. Accessed on: Mar. 20, 2019.

4 Now write the words from the box next to their definition.

Legend	Mythical	Devices	Beast

a. ____________: something imaginary or not real

b. ____________: a nonhistorical or unverifiable story

c. ____________: any nonhuman animal

d. ____________: mechanical or electrical inventions

#DAY65

DUBLIN, IRELAND

Can You Lend Me Your Tablet?

Tina: Come on, roommates, let's go sightseeing!

Kintaro: Just a second, let me grab my backpack.

Joanna: Hey, Tina, is this your tablet?

Tina: Yes, it's mine.

Joanna: My tablet is dead. I forgot to charge the battery. Can you lend me yours?

Tina: Sure!

Kintaro: Guys, do you think we will have time to visit the elegant Georgian houses?

Tina: Not today, Kintaro. But the guys from the other hostel invited us to visit the Georgian houses with them tomorrow.

Kintaro: It would be great to join them!

Joanna: Let's just hope it doesn't rain much while we are here.

Tina: I also heard it rains a lot here during the year. But Ireland is a wonderful country anyway!

Igor RAS/Arquivo da editora

Ireland

Capital: Dublin
Location: Northern Europe
Area: 70,273 sq. km
Population: 4,836,531
Currency: Euro
Languages: English, Irish Gaelic
Nationality: Irish

Mapa e bandeira: Banco de imagens/Arquivo da editora

The first known settlers at Dublin were Norsemen, or Vikings, who landed in the ninth century. Ireland is politically divided into Republic of Ireland, with Dublin as its capital, and into Northern Ireland, part of the United Kingdom, whose capital is Belfast.

GEORGIAN HOUSES, DUBLIN.

1 Answer the following questions.

a. Who were the first known settlers at Dublin?

____

b. How is Ireland politically divided?

____

2 Underline the correct words according to the dialog.

a. Tina wants to go **sightseeing/sleeping**.

b. Joanna asked **Tina/Kintaro** if **he/she** could lend the tablet to **him/her**.

c. Kintaro wants to visit the **decadent/elegant** Georgian houses.

3 Read Tina's e-mail and fill in the blanks with the correct words.

soon | a lot | kings | roommates | friendly | such | because

To: Lisa

From: Tina

Hi there!

Well, here I am in Ireland. It's _______ a pleasant place, with _______ people, but it seems to rain _______. It's very nice to go sightseeing with my _______ from the hostel. They are fun! Did you know that the Georgian houses we see here are named this way _______ they were built when the _______ on the throne of England had the name George? Isn't it interesting, Lisa?

I miss you and I'll show you all my pictures as _______ as I get back.

XX

Tina

#DAY82

PARIS, FRANCE

At the Tour Agency

Tina: *Bonjour*, do you speak English?

Attendant: Yes, madam. Can I help you?

Tina: I came here yesterday and the agency was closed.

Attendant: Oh, yesterday was a holiday in France.

Tina: I didn't know that! Can you give me an idea of what Paris has to offer?

Attendant: Sure, we have these folders with some suggestions.

Tina: May I have one?

Attendant: Sure, it's yours. How long are you staying?

Tina: A week.

Attendant: You could visit the Louvre Museum, the Eiffel Tower, the Arch of Triumph and go sightseeing on the Seine River.

Tina: Thanks for the help.

Attendant: You're welcome. Have a nice stay!

Igor RAS/Arquivo da editora

France

Capital: Paris
Location: Western Europe
Area: 543,965 sq. km
Population: 67,200,000
Currency: Euro
Language: French
Nationality: French

Mapa e bandeira: Banco de imagens/Arquivo da editora

The Eiffel Tower, which is 324 meters high, is an iron tower of the nineteenth century located in Champ de Mars, in Paris. It became a global France icon and one of the most recognizable structures in the world. The Eiffel Tower is the most visited paid monument in the world, and millions of people climb the tower every year. Named after its designer, engineer Gustave Eiffel, it's the biggest tourist attraction in Paris.

1 Answer the questions.

Gimas/Shutterstock

a. How high is the Eiffel Tower?

____

b. According to the text, what is the most visited paid monument in the world?

____

c. Which is the biggest tourist attraction in your city?

____

____

THE EIFFEL TOWER.

2 Read Tina's texts to her family and fill in the blanks with the words from the box.

help

popular

interesting

gardens

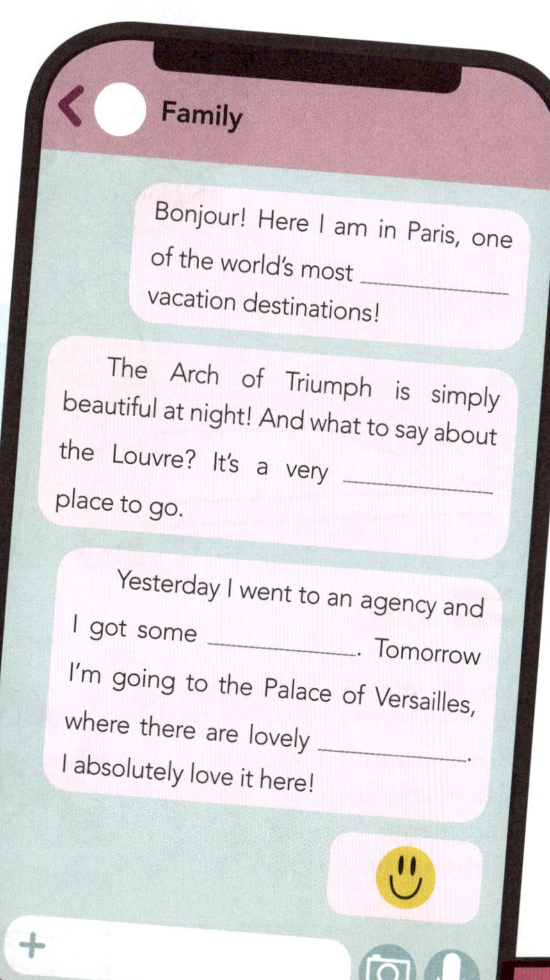

Family
Bonjour! Here I am in Paris, one of the world's most ____________ vacation destinations!
The Arch of Triumph is simply beautiful at night! And what to say about the Louvre? It's a very ____________ place to go.
Yesterday I went to an agency and I got some ____________. Tomorrow I'm going to the Palace of Versailles, where there are lovely ____________. I absolutely love it here!

Banco de imagens/Arquivo da editora

#DAY89

VIENNA, AUSTRIA

Going to a Concert

Tina: I'd like to buy a ticket for the Mozart Symphony Orchestra, please.

Attendant: What seat do you prefer?

Tina: A seat in the circle, please.

Attendant: Sorry, ma'am. There are no seats left in this area.

Tina: Upper circle?

Attendant: Yes. Here's the floor chart. You can choose your seat.

Tina: I will take C21. What time does the program start?

Attendant: At 9:30 p.m.

Tina: How much is it?

Attendant: It's 20 euros.

Tina: Here you are. Thanks.

Attendant: You're welcome.

Igor RAS/Arquivo da editora

Austria

Capital: Vienna
Location: Western Europe
Area: 83,879 sq. km
Population: 8,822,267
Currency: Euro
Language: German
Nationality: Austrian

Mapa e bandeira: Banco de imagens/Arquivo da editora

Haydn, Mozart, Beethoven, Schubert and Strauss – all of them famous composers – lived and worked in Vienna, which remains a center for classical music today.

Maryna Pleshkun/Shutterstock

THE VIENNA STATE OPERA.

1 Read and answer **T** (True) or **F** (False).

a. ◯ Tina got a seat in the circle.

b. ◯ The attendant showed Tina the floor chart.

c. ◯ The ticket's price is 25 euros.

d. ◯ Tina asked at what time the program starts.

2 Write the appropriate question to each of the following sentences.

a. Tina will watch the concert from the upper circle.

____

b. The ticket costs 20 euros.

____

c. Tina wants to watch the Mozart Symphony Orchestra.

____

3 Complete the text with the information from the brochure.

VIENNA MOZART ORCHESTRA

The Vienna Mozart Orchestra's repertoire ranges from all of Mozart's symphonies to a great variety of his instrumental concertos (for violin, piano and wind) to arias and duets from his most famous operas.

SCHEDULE:
Concerts from 2 May to 31 October.
Every Monday, Wednesday, Friday, and Saturday at 8:15 p.m.

CONCERT HALLS:
Golden Hall
Konzerthaus
Imperial Palace
Vienna Opera House

PRICES (EUR per person)	
VIP with dinner	300
superior	105
A	85
B	70
C	50

Book tickets online at www.viennatickets.com

Based on: <www.viennaticketoffice.com>. Accessed on: Mar. 20, 2019.

The Vienna Mozart Orchestra has a __________ of Mozart symphonies for __________, __________ and __________ from his most famous operas. The prices vary from __________EUR to __________ EUR with a meal included. The concerts can be at __________, Golden Hall, Konzerthaus, and Imperial Palace. The concerts take place from 2 May to 31 October, every Monday, Wednesday, Friday, and Saturday, always at __________.

#DAY120

BERLIN, GERMANY

What about a German Dessert?

Tina: *Hallo.*

Hans: *Hallo,* Tina! Is that you?

Tina: How did you guess?

Hans: 'Cause of your American accent. Are you in Berlin?

Tina: Yes! I'm at the Avantgarde Hotel.

Hans: Great! I know where it is. What about having a typical German meal tonight?

Tina: Oh! I like German food very much. But I'm really crazy about German desserts.

Hans: Great! Wait for me at 7 o'clock. Is that OK for you?

Tina: Done!

Hans: I'll come with a Brazilian friend called Carla, who I met here. She loves Berlin.

Tina: Great! I love Brazilian people. You rock, Hans!

Igor RAS/Arquivo da editora

Germany

Capital: Berlin
Location: Western Europe
Area: 357,168 sq. km
Population: 82,800,000
Currency: Euro
Language: German
Nationality: German

Mapa e bandeira: Banco de imagens/ Arquivo da editora

The tensions between East and West Berlin in 1961 culminated in the construction of a wall that separated the city. The Westerners could pass from one side to the other only through strictly controlled checkpoints. In 1989, the citizens from East Germany gained free access across the Berlin Wall, which was mostly demolished. In 1990, the two parts of the country were reunified as the Federal Republic of Germany, and Berlin became the German capital.

Shaun Higson/Berlin/Alamy/Fotoarena

FALL OF THE BERLIN WALL, 1989.

1 Read and complete the text.

The construction of the __________ was the result of __________ between __________ and __________. The __________ parts of the country were __________ in __________ as the Federal Republic of Germany.

2 Answer the following questions.

a. Where is Tina staying in Berlin? ______________________________

b. Does Tina like German food? ______________________________

3 Read and write the facts about Carla in the correct order.

www.hello!teens.com/Carlasblog

CARLA'S BLOG

ABOUT ME
GALLERY
OLD POSTS

My name is Carla, I was born in São Paulo, Brazil. I've been traveling since I was 15, when I first went to the US by myself to study one semester of my high school program. I graduated in 2008 and decided to go straight to Switzerland to take my MBA in Hospitality with Marketing Specialization. In 2012, I went to Berlin, in Germany, to study German. I had studied German in Brazil before, but it's always better to practice the language in the country of origin. I stayed there for 2 months in a house of a nice family, the Müller's, and learned a lot, not only about the language, but also about the German culture. When I came back to Brazil, I studied Hotel Management in São Paulo.

Thank you very much for spending some time reading about my life!

Carla D.

She went to Switzerland to do her MBA. Carla was born in São Paulo.
She studied Hotel Management in São Paulo.
She travelled to the United States to study one semester of high school.
In 2012, she went to Berlin, in Germany, to study German.

____

____

#DAY127

ATHENS, GREECE

I Need Towels and Soap, Please

Tina: Gee! Athens is the hottest city I've ever been to. Oh, no! I was thinking of taking a cold bath, but there is no towel or soap in the bathroom. I'm going to call room service.

Tina: The door is open. Please, come in.

Lady: Excuse me, madam. The towels and soap should be in the drawer. We forgot to put them there. But here they are. Is that all?

Tina: Yes, thank you.

Lady: You're welcome.

Igor RAS/Arquivo da editora

Greece

Capital: Athens
Location: Southern Europe
Area: 131,957 sq. km
Population: 11,100,000
Currency: Euro
Language: Greek
Nationality: Greek

Mapa e bandeira: Banco de imagens/ Arquivo da editora

Ancient Greeks believed Mount Olympus, the highest point in Greece, was the home of gods. The early Greeks were responsible for the first governments that were elected by people; so we can say that they invented democratic government.

johzio/Shutterstock

THE MOUNT OLYMPUS.

1 Read and answer the questions.

a. For the ancient Greeks, where was the home of gods?

____

b. Which people were responsible for creating the democratic government?

____

2 Now, answer according to the dialog.

a. What city in Greece is Tina visiting?

____

b. According to Tina, how is the temperature there?

____

3 Read the touristic leaflet and find the items in the text.

4-day Iconic
AEGEAN CRUISE

NAN728/Shutterstock

Round trip cruise from
Piraeus (Athens), Greece

Departs on Monday at 11:00 a.m. and returns on Friday at 6:00 a.m.

Dates are in March, April, May, June, July, August, September, October.

Ports of call: Piraeus (Athens), Greece/Mykonos, Greece/Kusadasi (Ephessos), Turkey/Patmos, Greece/Rhodes, Greece/Crete (Heraklion), Greece/Santorini, Greece

Spend a week on-board in the comfortable "Celestyal Olympia", visiting five of the most famous Greek islands, including a full day on the island of the Knights, Rhodes.

Based on: <www.dolphin-hellas.gr/cruises-greece/louis-cruises/>. Accessed on: Mar. 20, 2019.

a. The departure and the returning dates.

____

____

b. The port stops.

____

____

____

c. Number of islands to visit.

____

d. Name of the ship.

____

#DAY206

VALLETTA, MALTA

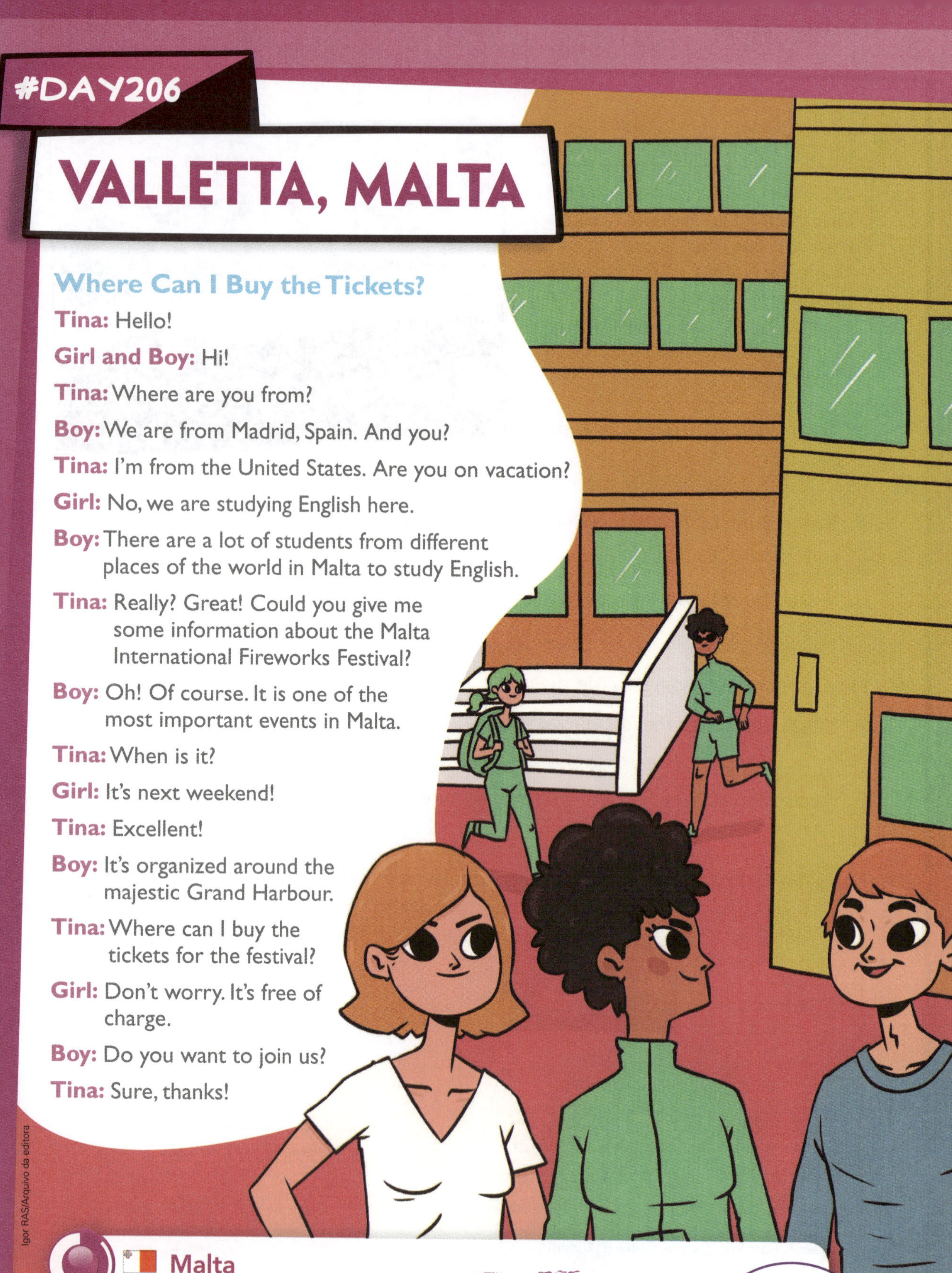

Where Can I Buy the Tickets?

Tina: Hello!

Girl and Boy: Hi!

Tina: Where are you from?

Boy: We are from Madrid, Spain. And you?

Tina: I'm from the United States. Are you on vacation?

Girl: No, we are studying English here.

Boy: There are a lot of students from different places of the world in Malta to study English.

Tina: Really? Great! Could you give me some information about the Malta International Fireworks Festival?

Boy: Oh! Of course. It is one of the most important events in Malta.

Tina: When is it?

Girl: It's next weekend!

Tina: Excellent!

Boy: It's organized around the majestic Grand Harbour.

Tina: Where can I buy the tickets for the festival?

Girl: Don't worry. It's free of charge.

Boy: Do you want to join us?

Tina: Sure, thanks!

Igor RAS/Arquivo da editora

Malta

Capital: Valletta
Location: Southern Europe
Area: 315,2 sq. km
Population: 500,000
Currency: Euro
Languages: Maltese, English
Nationality: Maltese

Valletta

Mapa e bandeira: Banco de imagens/Arquivo da editora

sam357/Shutterstock

The Fireworks Festival offers firework displays designed by foreign pyrotechnic companies as well as some of the best local fireworks factories. For each category, there is a trophy and a prize money to be won. Everyone is invited to attend and enjoy the spectacle. The festival celebrates Malta's accession into the European Union on May 1st, 2004.

GRAN HARBOUR.

1 What does the Fireworks Festival offer?

____

____

2 Match the expressions to their meanings.

a. free of charge ( ) pyrotechnic show
b. tickets ( ) no charge
c. fireworks show ( ) used to enter events

3 Answer the following questions.

a. Where is Tina going to go next weekend?

____

b. Does Tina need to buy a ticket? Why (not)?

____

c. Where is the festival organized?

____

4 Complete the sentences with information from the text.

a. Lots of students from different countries go to Malta to study ______________.

b. The ______________________ is one of the most important events in Malta.

c. People don't need ______________ for the Fireworks Festival.

d. The Fireworks Festival takes place around the ______________________.

LET'S LEARN MORE ABOUT EUROPE

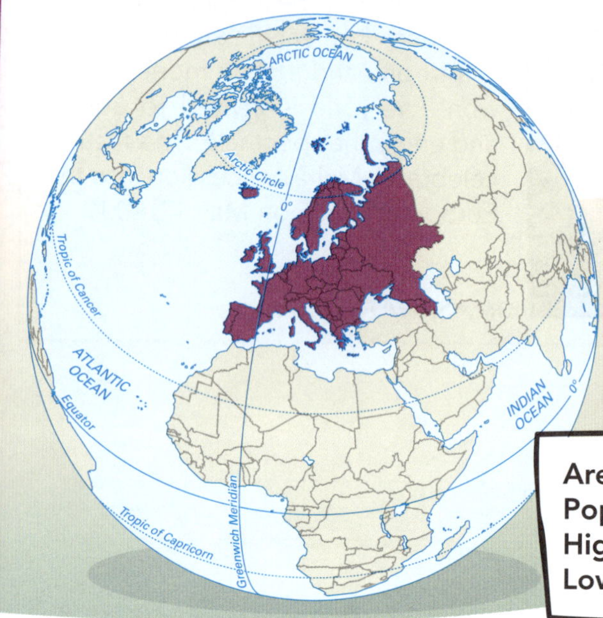

Europe is one of the world's seven continents.

Igor RAS/Arquivo da editora

Area: 10,390,000 sq. km
Population: 742,972,787
Highest point: Mount Elbrus, Russia (5,642 m)
Lowest point: Caspian Sea (–28 m)

Europe is connected to Asia, which is another continent. Bounded to the north by the Arctic Ocean, to the west by the Atlantic Ocean and to the south by the Mediterranean Sea. Europe's eastern frontier is vague, but has traditionally been given as the boundary betweeen the Ural Mountains and the Caspian Sea to the southeast.

Europe is also used as a short-form for the European Union (EU), the largest political and economic entity covering part of the European continent. The European Union currently comprises 27 member states.

Brent Wong/Shutterstock

THE PARTHENON, IN GREECE.

Brett Andersen/Shutterstock

THE KILKENNY CASTLE, IN IRELAND.

Europe has a long history. Its culture has spread to many parts of the world. Across it, about 60 different languages are spoken. Many people there used to live in farms but nowadays they live in the cities. Many of these cities are famous and popular with tourists.

Millions of people visit Europe each year. The continent has some of the most famous buildings and structures, including many old churches and castles.

Aleksander Bolbot/Shutterstock

Europe has different landscapes. Some parts have hills and mountains, other parts are flat and have thick forests. Almost half of Europe is covered with forests. Another big part of the territory is covered with farmland. In places where it is really warm, such as Greece, people grow olives on farms called groves.

THE BIALOWIEZA FOREST, IN POLAND.

The forests are home to many plants and animals. The brown bear lives in forests and it's found all over Europe in wooded areas. Reindeer live in the colder parts of Europe. They are very important to some groups of people that use the flesh of these animals for food and their skins for shelter and clothing. Some people also ride the reindeer to get around.

REINDEER ON THE ISLAND SENJA, NORWAY.

Juergen Ritterbach / Alamy/Fotoarena

Vaclav P3k/ Shutterstock

Europe is also known for its mountains. They are usually cold, especially in the winter. The Alps are very famous. People all over the world go there to spend holidays and ski.

SWISS ALPS.

Based on: *My First Encyclopedia*. Lincolnwood, Publications International, 2007.

ENGLAND

LONDON

s4svisuals/Shutterstock

THE BIG BEN.

What is the difference between the United Kingdom, Great Britain, and England?

The United Kingdom is a country that consists of Great Britain, formed by England, Wales and Scotland, and Northern Ireland. In fact, the official name of the country is "United Kingdom of Great Britain and Northern Ireland."

London is the capital of England and also the capital of the UK (United Kingdom). It's a great political and commercial center and a paradise for people who like good entertainment and shopping, but it's also a very quiet place with its parks and ancient buildings, and a capital of culture with its museums and libraries. Every day, at 11:30 a.m., at the gates of the Buckingham Palace, the residence of the queen, you can see the Changing of the Guard.

The city is known for its famous sights as the Big Ben, the Westminster Abbey and the Tower Bridge. Visitors enjoy taking the tube to explore the city and spend some hours in the great green areas, as the Hyde Park.

Based on: <http://geography.about.com/library/faq/blqzuk.htm>. Accessed on: Mar. 20, 2019.

1 Complete the sentences according to the text.

a. London is the capital of ____________________ and of the ____________________.

b. The Changing of the Guard occurs ____________________ at 11:30 a.m.

c. The United Kingdom is a country that consists of ____________________ and Northern Ireland.

d. The queen lives in Buckingham ____________________.

SCOTLAND

EDINBURGH

Bailey-Cooper Photography/Alamy/Fotoarena

THE EDINBURGH CASTLE.

The history of Scotland is fascinating. It once belonged to the Roman Empire, until the arrival of the Vikings. They forged a new kingdom where Macbeth ruled as King of Alba until 1057. It was only in 1707 that Scotland got closer to Britain by the creation of a single Parliament of the United Kingdom of Great Britain.

Edinburgh is the capital of Scotland. The city is dominated by Edinburgh Castle, built on a rock of volcanic origin. The city has one of the most prestigious universities of Europe and of the world, the University of Edinburgh, a pioneer in computer science and management.

The country was established as a cultural powerhouse as it was the location for several movies and home for the successful writer J.K. Rowling.

Based on: <www.scotland.org/about-scotland/history-timeline>.
Accessed on: Mar. 20, 2019.

1 Match the two parts of the sentences.

a. Macbeth ruled Scotland ( ) is Edinburgh.

b. The capital of the country ( ) on a volcanic rock.

c. J.K. Rowling wrote ( ) until 1057.

d. Edinburgh Castle is ( ) in Scotland.

2 Which movies were filmed in Scotland? Research and find out.

____

____

____

IRELAND

DUBLIN

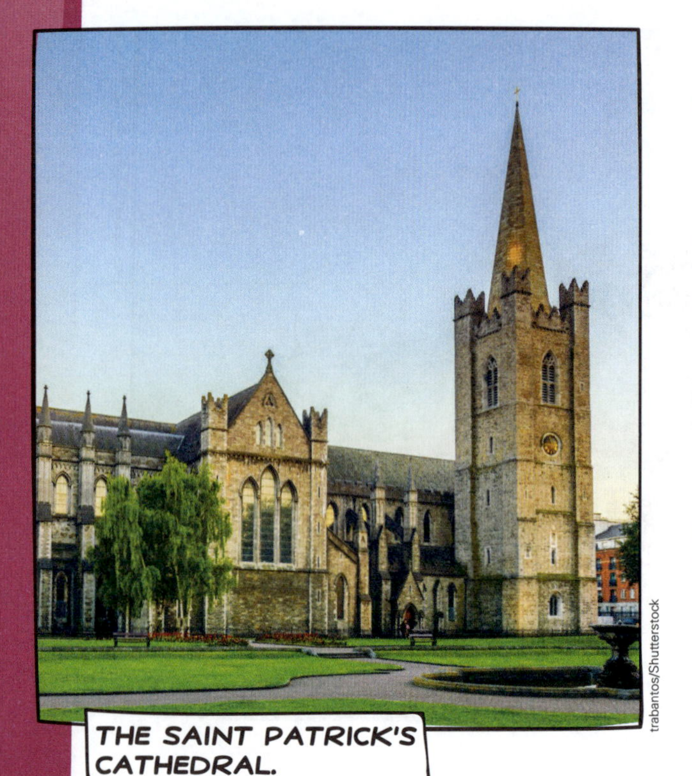

THE SAINT PATRICK'S CATHEDRAL.

trabantos/Shutterstock

Ireland is an island on the western edge of Europe. The capital city of the Republic of Ireland is Dublin. The country is a constitutional democracy and is a member of both the United Nations and the European Union.

Ireland is politically divided into Eire, or Republic of Ireland, and Northern Ireland, or Ulster. The island of Ireland is also called the Emerald Isle, because of its beautiful green countryside. The poetic name for the island is Erin. Gaelic is the original language of Ireland and the Gaelic name for Ireland is Eire. The first inhabitants were the Gaels and the Celts.

In the 5th century A.D., St. Patrick, the Patron Saint of Ireland, brought Christianity to Ireland. Saint Patrick's Cathedral and Dublin Castle are important buildings, both originally from 12th century.

Ireland is an English-speaking country, people speak both English and the Irish language (Irish Gaelic). It is well known for being friendly and safe. There is a large international student population, studying in various disciplines, at each of the universities and institutes of technology that are dotted all over the country.

Dublin is a thriving commercial and social center. Multinational software companies rest beside 500-year-old pubs where traditional music continues to flourish. Dublin has a rich literary history, with natives Jonathan Swift, Oscar Wilde, Seamus Heaney, Bernard Shaw, W. B. Yeats, James Joyce and Samuel Beckett, making Dublin the only city to host three Nobel Prize-winning writers.

Based on: <www.atlanticbridge.com/living-in-ireland>. Accessed on: Mar. 20, 2019.

1 Answer the following questions.

a. How is Ireland politically divided?

____

b. Describe Dublin.

____

c. Which languages do people speak there?

____

2 Complete the sentences according to the text.

a. The first inhabitants of Ireland were the __________ and the __________.

b. In the 5th century, St. Patrick brought Christianity to __________.

c. Two important buildings in Dublin are __________ and __________.

FRANCE

PARIS

Thierry Ougen/Getty Images

THE SEINE RIVER.

Paris is the capital of France and is located in the north of the country. It has been one of Western Europe's major centers of culture and business for a long time. Some of the world's greatest artists, writers, fashion designers and chefs have lived in Paris. The city is also famous for its beauty. The Seine River flows through the city center.

The French consider cooking an art, so if you are eating in France be prepared for a lot of food – and good food.

Paris industries also produce items such as perfume, fur, gloves, toys, clothing, and other goods. Heavy industries are situated in the suburbs. These include the manufacture of automobiles, machine tools, electric and electronic products, chemicals, and processed foods.

Tourism is one of the city's largest source of economy. One of Europe's most visited city, Paris is called the "City of Lights".

Based on: <http://kids.britannica.com/elementary/article-345991/Paris>. Accessed on: Mar. 20, 2019.

1 Answer the following questions.

a. Where is Paris located?

____

b. What do industries in Paris produce?

____

c. How is Paris called?

____

2 Write **T** (True) or **F** (False) according to the text.

a. ◯ The manufacture of automobiles is one of the city's most important source of economy.

b. ◯ In Paris heavy industries are situated downtown.

c. ◯ Paris is the home of many fashion designers.

AUSTRIA

VIENNA

Vienna has one of Europe's richest musical heritages: Mozart, Beethoven, Schubert, Brahms, Bruckner, Mahler, Schönberg, and Richard Strauss all lived and worked in the Austrian capital.

The Vienna Mozart Orchestra was founded in 1986 by 30 musicians from the best and most famous Viennese orchestras. They devoted themselves exclusively to the works of Wolfgang Amadeus Mozart and perform the concerts in historical costumes.

This and the typical Viennese atmosphere contribute to create an ambience which makes the audience feel as though they have stepped back to the end of the 18th century, period in which Mozart lived there.

A Brazilian woman born in Piauí directs this whole business. Her name is Amparo, but in Vienna she is known as Maria Grünbacher. Her husband, Gerald Grünbacher, was born in Austria and is a notorious musician there. He plays the clarinet in the Vienna Orchestra and in other important orchestras.

Based on: <www.viennaconcerts.com/mozart.php>. Accessed on: Mar. 20, 2019.

robertharding/Alamy/Fotoarena

INSIDE VIEW OF VIENNA STATE OPERA.

1 Answer the following questions.

a. List the names of some composers who lived and worked in Vienna.

____

____

b. Name the orchestra in which musicians devote themselves exclusively to the works of Mozart.

____

c. Who directs the business of the Vienna Mozart Orchestra?

____

2 Underline the correct alternative according to the text.

a. Gerald Grünbacher is **a Brazilian/an Austrian** notorious musician.

b. **Mozart/Picasso** is the most important composer born in Austria.

c. Wolfgang Amadeus Mozart lived in the **18th/19th** century.

GERMANY

BERLIN

Berlin is the capital of Germany as well as a city state, an autonomous federal state and the second largest city in the European Union.

Up-and-coming, dynamic and without restraint – Berlin is just larger than all other German towns and offers inexhaustible opportunities. From 1954 until 1989, the city was a divided city, but in 1990 it was reunited and became the capital of a united Germany.

Culture and leisure time: Berlin is famous for its theatrical landscape consisting of numerous theatres and cabarets. You will find lots of places in the city offering diverse opportunities, day and night, which are unique in Germany.

Patryk Kosmider/Shutterstock

THE BRANDENBURG GATE.

Music lovers can choose amongst Berlin Philharmonic Orchestra, Berlin State Opera, German Symphony Orchestra Berlin, and Berlin Radio Symphony Orchestra. The number of museums in the city is overwhelming, too. Moreover, there are the offices of lots of broadcasting companies and most German daily newspapers.

While soccer is clearly the national sport, cycling, tennis, track and field, car racing, horse racing, and boxing are practiced by a large number of people.

Based on: <www.europelanguagejobs.com/blog/what-makes-berlin-so-great.php>, <www.quora.com/What-is-it-like-to-live-in-Berlin>. Accessed on: Mar. 20, 2019.

1 Answer the following questions.

a. When did the division of Germany come to an end?

____

b. What is Berlin famous for?

____

____

c. What are the favorite sports of German people?

____

____

2 Underline the correct words according to the text.

a. In 1990, Berlin was **separated/reunited** and became the capital of a united Germany.

b. **Boxing/Soccer** is the national sport.

c. There is a great number of **museums/clubs** in Berlin.

GREECE

ATHENS

Scott E Barbour/Getty Images

ACROPOLIS OF ATHENS.

The city with the most glorious history in the world, Athens is worshipped by gods and people as a magical city. The enchanting capital of Greece has always been a birthplace for civilization. It's the city where democracy and most of the wise men of ancient times were born. The most important civilization of ancient world flourished in Athens. Who hasn't heard of the Acropolis of Athens?

Athens is a city of different aspects. A walk around the famous historic triangle (Plaka, Thission, Psyri), the old neighborhoods, reveal the coexistence of different eras. Old mansions, well-preserved ones and other worn down by time. Luxurious department stores and small intimate shops, fancy restaurants and traditional taverns. All have their place in this city.

Athens has the most important archaeological monuments – the Acropolis, Odeion of Herodes Atticus, Olymbion, Roman Market, Panathenaic Stadium or Kallimarmaro, The Temple of Poseidon in Sounion etc. In the capital, there is also the Greek Parliament, Athens Academy and University, the Archaeological Museum, Military Museum, Byzantine Museum etc.

Based on: <www.greece-athens.com/>. Accessed on: Mar. 20, 2019.

1 Answer the following questions.

a. What's the importance of Athens? Explain.

____

____

____

____

b. What are the city's most important cultural attractions?

____

____

____

____

2 Complete the sentences according to the text.

a. Athens is a city of ______________ aspects.

b. There are important archaeological ______________ in Athens.

MALTA

VALLETTA

Leonid Andronov/Shutterstock

MARSAMXETT HARBOUR.

People that visit Malta explore 7000 years of history in the islands that are described as a big open-air museum. Much of the past history is visible today, as you can retrace the footsteps of St. Paul or see where the Knights of St. John defended Christendom.

There are many outdoor activities as the sun shines almost all year long. In 48 hours in the island, you can try a new sport, go on a cruise or tour the most important historic sites.

As Malta was a British colony for more than 160 years, this legacy explain why English is one of the two official languages of the country. And with the excellent climate and offering the option of learning and vacationing, Malta is the ideal place to study English. You'll have the opportunity to practice the language in different situations as English is in newspapers, books, magazines, TV and radio channels. Most of the island's cultural programs are also in English.

Based on: <www.visitmalta.com/en/see-and-do>; <www.visitmalta.com/en/language-learning>. Accessed on: Mar. 20, 2019.

1 Complete the sentences with information from the text.

a. You can study ________ in Malta.

b. Malta was a ________ colony.

c. The country has more than 7000 years of ________.

d. You can go on a ________ in Malta.

2 Answer the questions.

a. How many languages do people speak in Malta?

____

b. Why do people speak English in Malta?

____

GLOSSARY

a lot: muito
about: sobre
accent: sotaque
access: acesso
accession: ascensão
according to: de acordo com, segundo
across: através de
activity: atividade
affectionately: afetuosamente
after: após, depois
again: novamente
agency: agência
all over: por toda parte
almost: quase
along: ao longo de
also: também
always: sempre
ambience: ambiente
ancient: antigo
announce: anunciar
another: outro/a
answer: responder
anyway: assim mesmo
appropriate: apropriado/a
April: abril
archaeological: arqueológico/a
aria: ária (peça musical)
around: ao redor de
arrival: chegada
as well as: assim como
ask: perguntar
aspect: aspecto
associate: associar
atmosphere: atmosfera
attend: assistir a
attendant: atendente
attraction: atração
audience: público
August: agosto
automobile: carro
autonomous: autônomo/a

backpack: mochila
bad: mau; má
bagpipes: gaita de foles
bank: margem
bath: banho
bathroom: banheiro
battery: bateria
be born: nascer
bear: urso; suportar
beast: besta, monstro
beautiful: bonito/a
beauty: beleza
because: porque
become: tornar-se
before: antes
begin: iniciar
believe: acreditar
belong: pertencer
beside: ao lado
(the) best: o/a melhor
better: melhor
between: entre
birthplace: local de nascimento
blank: vazio/a
block: quadra
boat: barco
book: reservar
both: ambos
boxing: boxe
bring: trazer
broadcast: transmitir
brochure: livreto
brown: marrom
build: construir
building: edifício, prédio
business: negócios
but: mas
buy: comprar
by the way: a propósito

call: chamar
career: carreira
castle: castelo
category: categoria
cathedral: catedral
celebrate: comemorar
center: centro
century: século
certainly: certamente
change: trocar
channel: canal
charge: carregar
chart: gráfico
check: controle
checkpoint: posto de controle ou de verificação
chef: chefe de cozinha
chemical: produto químico
choose: escolher
church: igreja
circle: circular; círculo
citizen: cidadão/cidadã
city: cidade
clarinet: clarinete
classical: clássico/a
climb: subir; escalar
close: fechar; próximo
clothing: vestuário
coast: costa
coexistence: coexistência
cold: frio/a
come: vir
come back: retornar
come on: vamos lá
comfortable: confortável
commercial: comercial
company: empresa
comparable: comparável
composer: compositor/a
comprise: abranger
concert: concerto
connect: ligar, conectar
consider: considerar
consist of: consistir em
construction: construção
contain: conter
continent: continente
contribute: contribuir
control: controlar
cook: cozinhar
costume: traje típico; fantasia
country: país
cover: cobrir
crazy: louco/a
creation: criação
creature: criatura
cruise: cruzeiro
culminate: culminar
culture: cultura
curiosity: curiosidade
currency: moeda
currently: atualmente

dark: escuro/a
dead: morto/a
decide: decidir
deep: profundo/a
defend: defender
democracy: democracia
democratic: democrático/a
demolish: demolir
depart: partir
dessert: sobremesa
destination: destino
device: dispositivo
devote: dedicar
difference: diferença
different: diferente
dinner: jantar
direct: dirigir
discipline: disciplina
discover: descobrir
display: apresentação; mostruário
diverse: diverso/a
divide: dividir
door: porta
(be) dotted: estar espalhado/a
downtown: centro da cidade
drawer: gaveta
duet: dueto
during: durante
dynamic: dinâmico/a

each: cada
early: cedo, primeiro/a
east: leste
eastern: oriental
economic: econômico/a
economy: economia
edge: borda, margem
eight: oito
eighteen: dezoito
elect: eleger
electric: elétrico/a
electronic: eletrônico/a
elegant: elegante
eleven: onze
emerge: emergir; surgir
enchanting: encantador/a
end: fim
enjoy: gostar de; curtir
entertainment: diversão, entretenimento
entity: entidade
establish: estabelecer
event: acontecimento, evento
every: todo; cada
everyone: todos/todas
excellent: excelente
exchange: trocar
exchange house: casa de câmbio
exclusively: exclusivamente
expedition: expedição
experience: vivenciar
expert: especialista
exploration: exploração
explore: explorar
expression: expressão
eye: olho

fact: fato
factory: fábrica
false: falso/a
family: família
famous: famoso/a
fancy: luxuoso/a
far away: distante, longe
farm: fazenda

farmland: terra cultivável
fascinating: fascinante
fashion: moda
feel: sentir
festival: festa; festival
fifteen: quinze
film: filmar
find: encontrar
find out: descobrir
fireworks: fogos de artifício
first: primeiro/a
five: cinco
flat: plano
floor: andar
flourish: prosperar
flow: fluir
following: seguinte
food: comida
footstep: passo
foreign: estrangeiro/a
forest: floresta
forget: esquecer
four: quatro
fourteen: quatorze
free: livre
free of charge: gratuito/a
Friday: sexta-feira
friend: amigo/a
friendly: amigável; simpático/a
frontier: fronteira
full: cheio/a; repleto/a
fun: divertido/a
fur: pelo; pele (animal)

gain: ganhar
garden: jardim
gate: portão
get back: voltar
give: dar
glorious: magnífico/a
glove: luva
go: ir
gods: deuses
goods: bens; produtos
government: governo
grab: agarrar; pegar
graduate: formar-se
great: ótimo/a
grove: pomar; bosque
grow: cultivar
guard: guarda
guess: adivinhar
guy: rapaz

half: metade
hall: entrada
harbour: porto
hear: ouvir
heart: coração
heavy: pesado/a
height: altura
help: ajudar
here: aqui
heritage: patrimônio
high: alto
high school: escola secundária, de ensino médio
hill: colina
history: história
holiday: feriado
home: lar
hope: esperar; esperança
hostel: albergue
hot: quente
house: casa
how: como
husband: marido

icon: ícone
iconic: icônico/a
in fact: na verdade
inaugurated: inaugurado/a
include: incluir
including: inclusive; incluindo
industry: indústria
inexhaustible: inesgotável
inhabitant: habitante
instruction: instrução
interesting: interessante
into: em
invent: inventar
invite: convidar
iron: ferro
island: ilha

join: reunir-se com
July: julho
June: junho
just: só, apenas

kilt: saia masculina típica da Escócia e da Irlanda
king: rei
kingdom: reino
know: conhecer; saber

lake: lago
land: aterrissar; terra
landmark: marco
landscape: paisagem
language: idioma
large: grande
later: mais tarde
leaflet: folheto
learn: aprender
legacy: legado
legend: lenda
leisure: lazer
lend: emprestar
let's: vamos
library: biblioteca
life: vida
light: luz
like: gostar
literally: literalmente
live: viver
locate: estar localizado/a
location: localização
lock: trancar
long: comprido/a, longo/a
look for: procurar
love: amar; adorar
lovely: encantador/a; lindo/a
low: baixo/a
luck: sorte
luxurious: luxuoso/a

machine: máquina
madam/ma'am: senhora
magazine: revista
major: principal
make: fazer
man: homem
management: administração
mansion: mansão
manufacture: fabricar
March: março
May: maio
meal: refeição
meet: encontrar
member: membro
message: mensagem
meter: metro
million: milhão
mine: meu/minha
miss: sentir falta de
Monday: segunda-feira
month: mês
monument: monumento
mostly: em geral
mount: monte
mountain: montanha
movie: filme
much: muito/a
museum: museu
music: música
my: meu/minha
myself: mim (mesmo/a)
myth: mito
mythical: imaginário/a

name: nome; nomear
national: nacional
nationality: nacionalidade
native: nativo/a
near: perto
neck: pescoço
need: necessitar, precisar
neighborhood: vizinhança
new: novo/a
newspaper: jornal
next: próximo/a
nice: simpático/a; agradável
night: noite
nine: nove
nineteen: dezenove
nineteenth: décimo nono
ninth: nono
north: norte
northern: do norte, setentrional
northwest: noroeste
notorious: famoso/a
now: agora
nowadays: hoje em dia

occur: acontecer
ocean: oceano
October: outubro
offer: oferecer; oferta
old: velho/a
olive: azeitona
on-board: a bordo (de)
once: uma vez
one: um
only: somente
open: abrir
opportunity: oportunidade
orchestra: orquestra
order: pedir; ordem
organize: organizar
origin: origem
originally: no princípio
other: outro/a
outdoor: ao ar livre
over: sobre
overwhelming: enorme

palace: palácio
paradise: paraíso
park: parque
pass: passar
password: senha
pay: pagar
people: pessoas; povo
perform: apresentar
person: pessoa
photograph: fotografar
physician: médico/a

piano: piano
picture: foto
pioneer: pioneiro/a
place: lugar
plant: planta
play: tocar
pleasant: agradável; simpático/a
poetic: poético/a
point: ponto
political: político/a
politically: politicamente
port: porto
pound: libra
powerhouse: potência
practice: praticar
prefer: preferir
prestigious: prestigioso/a
price: preço
prize: prêmio
processed: processado/a
product: produto
program: programar; programa
pub: bar
put: colocar
pyrotechnic: pirotecnia; pirotécnico/a

queen: rainha
question: pergunta
quiet: sossegado/a; quieto/a

rain: chover
range: alcance; gama
read: ler
really: realmente
receptionist: recepcionista
recognizable: reconhecível
reindeer: rena
relate: relacionado/a
relax: relaxar
remain: permanecer
remind: lembrar
repertoire: repertório
residence: residência
responsible: responsável
restraint: restrição
result: resultado
retrace: refazer
return: retornar
reunited: unir novamente
reveal: revelar
rich: rico/a
ride: montar; viagem
river: rio
rock: pedra
room: quarto
room service: serviço de quarto
roommate: colega de quarto
round trip: viagem de ida e volta
rule: governar; regra

safe: cofre; seguro
Saturday: sábado
schedule: horário
science: ciência
scientific: científico/a
sea: mar
search: procurar
seat: assento
second: segundo/a
see: ver
seem: parecer
semester: semestre
sentence: frase
separate: separar
September: setembro
settler: colonizador
seven: sete
seventeen: dezessete
several: vários/várias
shelter: abrigo
shine: brilhar
show: mostrar
sightseeing: passeio turístico
sign: placa
simply: simplesmente
since: desde
single: único/a
situation: situação
six: seis
sixteen: dezesseis
ski: esquiar
skin: pele
skirt: saia
soap: sabonete; sabão
soccer: futebol
solo: desacompanhado/a
some: algum/alguma
song: canção
soon: cedo; em breve
source: fonte
south: sul
southeast: sudeste
southern: do sul, meridional
speak: falar
spectacle: espetáculo
spend: gastar
sport: esporte
spread: propagar; espalhar
start: começar
state: estado
station: estação
stay: permanecer
still: ainda
straight: direto
strictly: estritamente
structure: estrutura
study: estudar
stuff: coisa
submarine: submarino
suburb: subúrbio
successful: bem-sucedido/a
such as: tal como
suggest: sugerir
supposedly: supostamente
sure: certamente
symbol: símbolo
symphony: sinfonia; sinfônica

tartan: xadrez escocês
tavern: taverna
tech: tecnologia
ten: dez
tension: tensão
them: eles/elas
there: lá
there is/are: há
these: estes/estas
thick: denso/a; espesso/a
think: achar; pensar
thirteen: treze
this: este/esta
though: embora
three: três
thriving: próspero/a
throne: trono
through: através de, por
ticket: ingresso
today: hoje
tomorrow: amanhã
tonight: esta noite
tool: ferramenta
tour: viagem
tourism: turismo
tourist: turista; turístico/a
towel: toalha
tower: torre
toy: brinquedo
track and field: atletismo
traditionally: tradicionalmente
travel: viajar
tree: árvore
triangle: triângulo
trip: viagem
trophy: troféu
true: verdadeiro/a
trunk: tronco
try: tentar; experimentar
tube: metrô
twelve: doze
twenty: vinte
two: dois
type: tipo
typical: típico/a

under: sob; abaixo
underground: metrô
underline: sublinhar
unique: único/a
university: universidade
until: até
up-and-coming: promissor/a
upper: superior
usually: geralmente

vacation: férias
vague: vago/a
variety: variedade
vary: variar
very: muito/a
violin: violino
visible: visível
visit: visitar
visitor: visitante
volcanic: vulcânico/a

wait: esperar
walk: caminhar
wall: muro; parede
want: querer
warm: quente
way: caminho
wear: vestir
Wednesday: quarta-feira
week: semana
weekend: final de semana
well known: conhecido/a
west: oeste
western: ocidental
what: o que
what about...?: que tal?
wheel: roda
when: quando
where: onde
which: o/a qual
while: enquanto
who: quem
whole: todo
win: vencer
wind: instrumento de sopro
wise: sábio/a
with: com
woman: mulher
wonderful: maravilhoso/a
wooded: arborizado/a
work: trabalhar
world: mundo
worry: preocupar-se
worship: venerar
writer: escritor/a

year: ano
yesterday: ontem
you're welcome: de nada